Conversation Starters for Every Grandparent

Conversation Starters for Every Grandparent

Tips for Talking to (and with) Your Grandchildren, Your Children, and Other Grandparents

Kim Chamberlain

Skyhorse Publishing

Skyhorse Publishing books may be purchased in bulk at special discounts for sales promotion, corporate gifts, fund-raising, or educational purposes. Special editions can also be created to specifications. For details, contact the Special Sales Department, Skyhorse Publishing, 307 West 36th Street, 11th Floor, New York, NY 10018 or info@skyhorsepublishing.com.

Skyhorse® and Skyhorse Publishing® are registered trademarks of Skyhorse Publishing, Inc.®, a Delaware corporation.

Visit our website at www.skyhorsepublishing.com.

10 9 8 7 6 5 4 3 2 1

Library of Congress Cataloging-in-Publication Data is available on file.

Cover design by Eve Siegel

Print ISBN: 978-1-63220-519-3
Ebook ISBN: 978-1-63220-897-2

Printed in the United States of America

TABLE OF CONTENTS

INTRODUCTION

Grandparents

I feel very fortunate to have known and spent time with three of my grandparents, my mum's parents and my dad's mother—sadly my dad's father died before I was born—and I feel even more fortunate to have had my mum's mother around until I was in my thirties.

I've always believed that Grandma, my dad's mother, was—if such a thing is possible—a saint on earth. At age 30 she went into the hospital for eye treatment; the doctor mistook her for another patient and gave her an injection in both eyes that made her lose her sight and become totally blind. Her response, incredibly, was "God bless him, anyone can make a mistake." In her sixties she lost the use of her legs and became bedridden until the end of her life at the age of 80. Unable to see or leave her bed, she accepted her fate comfortably and was forever kind and considerate. She was looked after by her sister, my great aunt Lena.

We used to visit Grandma and Aunty Lena every Sunday, but being a very shy youngster I rarely spoke to Grandma, possibly because I was never on my own with her. I see now what a huge loss that was, and if I could turn back the clock I would love to have spent more time with her, find out about her earlier life and her thoughts and views on the world. We could have had some very interesting conversations.

My mum's father, Gag (it was the nearest I could say to "granddad" when I was little and the name stuck), was a very practical person who would spend a lot of time in his shed doing "granddad" things like repairing shoes and making furniture, or in his room upstairs doing some very impressive calligraphy. He made me a dolls' house, and also calligraphy posters for my wall. One of the most special things he made for me was a tiny, tiny gold cardboard box, big enough to hold just one grain of rice on which he had written my name.

Nan, my mum's mother, took me under her wing from an early age and I used to spend a lot of time with her. She taught me Scottish Country Dancing in her living room; we would color in paper doilies together; and we would make bead curtains out of string, dark green beads and tiny, rolled up pieces of wallpaper. She was an avid bowls player and so I learned to play crown green bowls and accompanied her to tournaments.

For a special treat we would take a train to the beach 20 miles away, collect cockle shells, come home, paint them and then use them to decorate plant pots.

Sometimes on a Saturday Nan would go to the local shops, then come to our house on the way back with her food shopping. She used to buy a big slice of cheese for my granddad and would break bits off the end to give to me. Then she would whisper "I won't tell your Gag that I've given you some of the cheese, I'll tell him the mice must have eaten the end of it." I thought that was very funny, and it was our special secret. I genuinely thought that Gag would believe the mice had eaten some of his cheese.

I wish I'd had a book like this when I was growing up, so that I could spend purposeful time with my grandparents where we found out more about each other and had some interesting discussions. I'd love to have known more about their childhood, their dreams, the world they grew up in, their chores around the house, what their parents were like, what their bedroom was like, the interesting incidents in their life, and their thoughts on various issues. Many of those were things I never thought to ask about, and although some of them cropped up in conversation from time to time, there is so much more about my grandparents I could have found out. I know it would have created a greater bond between us.

As you have a copy of this book, you most likely have a grandchild or grandchildren you'd like to have meaningful conversations with. How fortunate that you are in this situation where you can spend precious time chatting with your grandchildren. The bond between grandparent and grandchild can be a very special and enriching one for both parties.

And how wonderful for your grandchildren that they have grandparents who want to spend time with them. These times are very precious and you will be creating some very special memories together. Perhaps they will find out a lot of really cool stuff about you that they don't already know!

As a grandparent you may be fortunate to have time that parents, and especially single parents, don't. You may play a particular role, such as sharing the family history or sharing your skills, being an educator, a listener, an advisor, a provider of fun. Perhaps through conversation you can find other ways to enhance your role. And perhaps your grandchildren will play a very special role for you—maybe something as simple as being a listener to your stories—without even realizing it.

Why a conversation starters book specifically for grandparents?

Grandparents are a growing force. They comprise a large percentage of the population, are generally younger in age and outlook, and are having fuller lives than grandparents of the past. A large proportion of grandparents thoroughly enjoy the grandparenting role and love spending time with their grandchildren.

Purpose of the book

The main purpose of the book is to facilitate conversations between grandparents and grandchildren, bringing in a wide and varied range of topics to talk about, and in a range of different ways. The book makes the assumption that the grandparents and grandchildren have a fundamentally emotionally healthy relationship.

How well do you and your grandchildren know each other? Conversation starters can stimulate communication and touch on topics that you may not have thought of. They can help you find out how interesting the other person is!

Grandchildren can ask their grandparents questions to find out more about them, their views, their ideas, and their preferences.

Equally, grandparents can ask their grandchildren questions to find out more about them and their views, as well as jointly making up stories or fun scenarios together, and doing activities that can lead to some interesting learning about each other.

However, while being a grandparent includes grandchildren it also includes a lot more. This book respects the different aspects of life that are present now that you have reached the stage of being a grandparent. It gives you the opportunity to look at other topics through conversations you can have with your children, your partner, your friends, and others, not only about grandparenting, but also about other facets of your life, and issues facing grandparents today. For example: your relationship, plans for the future, family challenges, issues regarding aging, travel, money, work or business, and fun!

A very easy book to dip into, *Conversation Starters for Every Grandparent* is suitable for grandparents, parents, grandchildren, and friends of grandparents and contains conversation starter topics that are warm, loving, interesting, thought-provoking, silly, challenging, and fun.

They provide the opportunity for laughter, intellectual discussion, ways to deal with challenges, making plans, finding out more about each other, and especially the chance to building stronger connections with your family members and friends.

USING THE BOOK

A benefit of this book is that you can use it for as long or short a period as you like, either in one-on-one situations or when there are a few of you together. You can simply dip into it when you are with your grandchild, child, partner, or friends and want to have a light-hearted conversation, or you can set aside time and create the right environment if you want to discuss a more in-depth topic. Ultimately the aim is to use the conversation starters as a way to build deeper connections with others.

1. How the book is organized

The book comprises:

Speaking skills

This section contains suggested techniques for building speaking skills and enhancing conversations in general, and highlights issues to be aware of when having conversations with children.

Questions and conversation starters

The 1000 questions and conversation starters fall into five separate sections:

1. For grandchildren to ask their grandparents
2. For grandparents to ask their grandchildren
3. For grandparents to ask their adult children
4. For grandparent couples to ask each other
5. For grandparents in general conversation to ask fellow grandparents and other adults

The starters consist of 100 different topic areas, each containing ten questions or conversation starters.

The starters fall into many types of categories, including ones that are fact finding, "What is your favorite book?", ones that pose hypothetical questions, "If you were given $1000 what would you spend it on?", and ones that ask for others' views, "What kinds of films, TV programs, and books are not suitable for young children?". There are other ways conversations can start and so you will also find starters such as storytelling, activities, and questions posed to an advice columnist.

Sometimes you will find similar versions of the same starter in different categories, for example, a grandchild can ask a grandparent, "Did you like school?" while a grandparent can ask a grandchild, "What do you like best about your school?"

Towards the end of the book there is space for you to make a note of any of your favorite starters or to compile some of your own.

Quotes

Quotes have been sprinkled throughout the conversation starters, firstly for pleasure, and secondly as a way to provide interesting perspectives on issues. Quotes can provide new and different angles on topics, and can spark off ideas that may enhance conversations. They can help develop your thinking about an issue and perhaps give an outlook you hadn't considered before. They can also act as conversation starters in themselves, and may prompt some interesting discussions.

There are two hundred quotes on different topics by a wide variety of people. They fall into three categories:

- Quotes about grandparents, grandchildren, and children (GPCH)
- Quotes about couples (CP)
- Quotes about conversation (CN)

The letters (GPCH), (CP), or (CN) will be found in front of each quote.

Keepsake memories

At the end of the book are blank pages for you to make a note of the interesting points or stories arising from your conversations.

For example, since my children were small I've kept a note of some of the wonderful things they have said, and I love reading them and sharing them with the children. It produces much laughter. This is a conversation between my husband and our daughter when she was six years old:

Daughter: Dad, how old do you need to be before you'll be a granddad?
Husband: I don't need to be a particular age; something needs to happen before I become a granddad.
Daughter: What?
Husband: For me to be a granddad YOU need to do something. You need to have a ...?
Daughter: ... a bath?

Writing down anecdotes and interesting points from conversations will serve as a way of preserving special memories, and will be a source of pleasure when you look back on them in the future. You may like to pass on the book to your grandchildren as a memento.

2.   Suggestions for using the starters

The starters can be used with many people, and cover many topics, so there are a few things to bear in mind.

Choose appropriate starters

When using the starters with children, choose ones that are appropriate for the age of your grandchild.

For example, questions such as, "If your teddy or your favorite toy came to life, what would you do together?" would be used for younger grandchildren, while ones such as, "Do teenagers get bad publicity in the media, unfairly?" would be used for older grandchildren.

Amend the starters

Sometimes you can adapt the starters to fit with the circumstances. For example, for teenage grandchildren you could amend the starter, "What's the best thing about being a child?" to, "What's the best thing about being a teenager?" Or, if the question asks about mom and dad such as, "Let's pretend we have to make up a show to perform for your mom and dad. What shall we do?" and they only have one parent, simply amend it to fit the situation.

Or, in the Grandparent Couples section one of the starters is, "Do you feel as protective towards our grandchildren as you did towards our children?" This assumes the couple has the same children and grandchildren. If not, you could amend it to, "Do you feel as protective towards your grandchildren as you did towards your children?"

Use starters at appropriate times

Some of the starters may not be suited to beginning a "cold" conversation. For example, you might feel it's not appropriate to begin a conversation with your adult child with, "Is there anything I could do to be a better grandparent?" Or you may not want to start a conversation with another adult with one of the more challenging issues in the Advice Column sections. It may be better to create the right environment by starting a conversation with more general issues, then build up to more sensitive topics.

Create a safe environment

People will be unwilling to talk, and conversation is likely to shut down, if they feel they are going to be judged or have their contribution ridiculed or disputed in an unpleasant way.

Create a safe conversational environment where people feel that they, and their contributions, are valued and that they can trust that you and others will respect their views.

Sensitive issues

Be careful when talking about certain topics, as some may be sensitive issues for children or others. You do not have to use all the starters. If you feel the topic may cause people to feel upset or challenged, then simply move on to another starter; there are many to choose from.

Use them again

You can use some of the starters more than once. Some starters, such as Tell a Story or Joint Stories, easily lend themselves to being used more than once.

Some you can use at a later date—say months or even years later—and you may find you get a different response. For example: "Who is your best friend at school?" "What's the best thing about being a grandparent?" "What is something special about your grandchild that makes you proud of them?"

Types of starters

Most of the starters are questions or issues to discuss; however there are other ways that conversations can start, and so there are starters that are:

- Story starters, either stories for you to tell your grandchild, or joint stories you can make up together. You can learn a lot about a child from the stories they tell, the way they think, and the issues they bring into the story. Asking children to tell joint stories with you has additional benefits, as it allows them to use their imagination and creativity, works their memory, hones their listening skills, and develops confidence in speaking. The stories may also spark off new lines of conversation, or you can pick up on something your grandchild mentions and ask them about it at the end.
- Activities. There are suggested activities you can do with your grandchild, along with suggested topics to talk about while you are doing them. Some children (and adults!), especially those who are quiet or who are not naturally talkative, find it easier to have a conversation while focusing on something else, rather than focusing on having a conversation. You can use the activities for their own sake and let conversation arise naturally on any subject, or you could use them to bring up a specific topic you'd like to talk about. The activities provide the potential to start some interesting lines of conversation.
- Advice columns. These starters contain issues to discuss with other adults. In these sections you are to imagine that you're an advice columnist who specializes in giving advice to grandparents, and have to give your recommendations regarding the problems presented. The advice column technique is a way to look at actual or potential issues and how you might deal

with them by being one step removed. They can be useful ways to discuss how to tackle difficult issues such as illness, long distance grandparenting, and family challenges.

Practical uses

- For younger children, you will have to read out, or help read out, the questions they will be asking you.
- If children are old enough to read, you can invite them to read out the quotes included in the topics, as well as the starters. They may also serve as a conversation starter.
- You can work through the topics in any order. For example, you could choose one section at a time and work through all ten topics, or you could pick the first ones from a range of topics.
- You could keep the book handy, say in your bag or in the glove compartment of your vehicle, or you could write out a number of topics, or take a photo of them with your phone, and keep them with you to use when you are with your grandchildren or others.
- You could read through the starters, get a sense of the ones you would like to discuss, and keep them in the back of your mind for when an opportunity arises.
- You could specifically choose topics you are keen to discuss, and make time to have a conversation with your grandchild, child, partner, or friend, for example.
- If you and your grandchildren don't live near each other, is there another way you could use the conversation starters? For example, via phone calls, Skype, email…? Perhaps you could have a question a week.

Remember that no matter the topic, the main aim is to spend quality conversation time together and increase the bond between you.

SPEAKING SKILLS

A number of years ago I used to work with a woman who I'll call Rose. Rose was a very thoughtful and kind woman, and I liked her a lot. However, I worked out that I could only risk asking her a question if I had a long time to listen to her answer. A typical conversation might go along the lines of:

Rose: How was your weekend?
Me: Great, it was my grandmother's birthday on Saturday so we had the family round for lunch. My Nan really enjoyed it. How was your weekend?
Rose: Well…I decided that I was going to make a special meal for my husband and wanted to use a new recipe, so I got out a recipe book that I hadn't used for a long time and sat reading it for an hour. It's an old recipe book that my mother had given me, and there were so many recipes I'd forgotten about. Anyway I found a recipe that required asparagus and I knew I hadn't got any in, so decided to go to the local shops. I couldn't decide whether I should walk or take the car, so I asked my husband to check on the weather forecast. It didn't look too bad so I decided to walk. Well…do you know who I bumped into while I was walking to the shops? Old Mrs. Wilkinson! And can you believe that she's had an operation on her leg? She was walking quite awkwardly so I don't think the operation has been a success. I said to her, "I think you should go back and see the surgeon, you know, that leg doesn't look right to me," but she didn't want to listen and said everything was as it should be. I don't think she should be walking so awkwardly and I'm going to check up on her next week. So … when I got to the shops, the man in the greengrocer's … what's his name?

Phil? Paul? Pete? ... I can't remember now, but he's got brown hair and glasses and always looks clean-shaven ... anyway he was telling me about his daughter who had just come back from a skiing trip. And you'll never guess what happened. It was the most amazing thing ...

And on and on the story would go, twisting and turning all over the place.

Rose was a pleasant woman who enjoyed speaking, and so I would nod, smile, and laugh at all the appropriate moments; but from time to time I would think of the quote by poet Richard Armour, who said, "It is all right to hold a conversation but you should let go of it now and then."

We're all probably guilty of some conversational faux pas from time to time, and one of the issues that may hold us back is that we can only operate at our level of awareness. If we're not aware of what we are doing or are not aware of conversational techniques, then we won't be able to do anything to improve on our skills.

Rose may not have been aware that she tended to speak for very long periods at a time, and that her conversations had a habit of becoming monologues.

Let's have a look at some of the fundamental aspects of effective conversations—the rhythm of conversation, listening skills, and speaking skills:

Conversation techniques

1. The rhythm of conversation

Conversations are two-way interactions that consist of dialogue, not monologues. The rhythm of conversation is such that the focus of speaking and listening flows easily from one person to another, where the person speaking has the opportunity to say what they want to, and the people listening pay attention to the speaker's message.

To enable the easy flow of conversation, people need to firstly understand the concept of turn taking. Taking turns involves partici- pants contributing to the conversation.

Successful turn taking means:
* Speaking for some of the time.

- Knowing what to talk about—keeping on-topic and making appropriate contributions.
- Knowing how much to contribute—not taking up too much or too little speaking time.
- Knowing when to stop.
- Knowing how to pass the conversation over to another person.
- Being comfortable about all people having a share of the conversation time.

When taking turns, the people involved do not each need to speak for the same amount of time. A successful conversation is one where each person has the chance to contribute in a satisfactory way. This means that if people dominate a conversation or contribute very little (or perhaps not at all), this will generally not lead to a satisfactory conversation rhythm.

Effective communicators can signal turn taking in a number of ways, by, for example, pausing, looking at another person, changing their intonation, changing their body position, or asking a question.

Note that when someone tells a story, the usual turn-taking aspect of conversation stops and it's expected that the other person will listen to the whole story. Once the story has finished, normal turn-taking resumes. If you are the person telling the story, bear in mind that you shouldn't go off at too many tangents, nor tell a story that is too long to hold people's attention.

Secondly, the easy flow of conversation entails people being proficient at two skills:

- The skill to be able to engage another person in the conversation. Engaging another person is usually done by asking a question, preferably an open question. An open question is one that allows for a longer answer than a "Yes" or "No" response, for example, "What do you think?", "Where did you go at the weekend?", "What happened when you met up with Jonathon?" It also involves the questioner indicating to the other person they are interested in their response. This may be done by turning to face them, smiling, making eye contact, leaning forward slightly, looking attentive, asking questions to clarify, and so on.

- The skill to make their contribution both interesting for the listeners and one that will inspire other people to contribute when it's time for turn taking. This means that the person speaking always needs to hold in the back of their mind a respect for others and their desire to contribute, and therefore avoid talking in such a way that keeps the focus on themselves. For example, Rose's contribution to the conversation was aimed at keeping the focus on herself for a long time, and was not carried out in such a way that would necessarily inspire others to contribute. If she had, for example, spent an amount of time talking about the recipe she used, without going off at tangents, and then included a pause in her speaking, it may have led to me contributing a story about a new recipe I had also tried. That would have then been a conversational flow rather than a monologue.

2. Listening

The author Ernest Hemingway once said, "I like to listen. I have learned a great deal from listening carefully. Most people never listen."

Effective listening doesn't just happen, it's a skill that needs to be learned and honed. Being a competent listener is a very useful ability to acquire—it helps you learn; it helps people relate to you; it helps build good relationships, and it is also the basis for successful conversations.

Note that there is a difference between hearing and listening. Hearing is passive, while listening is active. To really understand a message means actively paying attention to what the other person is saying. It's not unusual for people to appear to be listening, when in fact they are simply waiting for their turn to speak, or have let their thoughts wander.

People want to be listened to. It is, unfortunately, quite common for people to feel that they are not adequately listened to; that they are interrupted; that their views are ignored; or that people are not listening to the essence of what they are saying.

The acronym S.T.A.Y. is a useful one to remember for effective communication; it stands for Stop Thinking About Yourself. The less you focus on yourself and what you want, and the more you focus on other people and their desire to be listened to, the better the conversationalist you will become.

What are some of the factors that can get in the way of good listening?

Remember that hearing is passive and listening is active, so if we don't focus on the act of listening, other factors may creep in:

- Not concentrating; letting your mind wander; daydreaming; tuning out.
- Misuse of spare time. We can listen approximately three times faster than people speak. How do you use this time? Do you use it to focus on the message or do you let your mind go elsewhere?
- Prejudging what people say: "I've heard it before," "They can't tell me anything new," "Their circumstances are just like X's."
- Mentally debating with the speaker; looking for weaknesses if we are knowledgeable in the area; mentally phrasing what we are going to say to look "clever."
- Prejudging the person or having a lack of empathy. If they look or sound different to you; if you feel little or no empathy; if they have irritating mannerisms.
- Letting emotions get in the way. People may use words or say things that cause strong emotions in you, and you may focus on these rather than the message.
- Missing the non-verbals. A large proportion of communication is non-verbal. Are you picking up on the whole message? Have you noticed any feelings that are being expressed, for example, via the other person's voice, facial expressions, or body language?
- Poor posture. If you slump in your seat or lean your head, for example, this can cause lack of oxygen to the brain and make focusing more difficult.

What are some of the ways we can develop our listening skills?

- Make a conscious decision to listen, tune in and focus on what the other person is saying, and give them your undivided attention. Deliberately decide to stop your mind from wandering by, for example, mentally summarizing from time to time what the other person has said. There are times when it's good to wait until they have stopped speaking before formulating a response. It may not be easy in the beginning, but with practice it will start to come more naturally.

- Show you are listening. To help keep the conversation flowing, use "minimal encouragers." These are small words, noises, or movements to show the other person you are listening to them and are encouraging them to carry on speaking. For example, you can look at them when they are speaking; tilt your head; nod your head; smile and lean slightly forward; or say things like "uh huh," "OK," or "yes." This indicates to the other person that you are interested in what they are saying, and that you want them to continue. Minimal encouragers are actions that people generally don't notice when they are present. However, if they are absent, people may have a general sense that something isn't right, or may assume you aren't interested or aren't listening.

- Show you are listening: have eye contact. Looking at the other person while they are speaking is a way to make conversation flow more easily. People like to feel that the other person is interested, and appropriate eye contact is one way to show this. It's also a mark of respect. Although people may say they can listen and do something else at the same time, the speaker would probably prefer your undivided attention. We all like being listened to. To have appropriate eye contact, look at the other person for the majority of the time, usually for around five seconds at a time, and then look elsewhere for a small amount of time. Avoid holding their gaze for too long so that it seems like you are staring at them, and also avoid holding their gaze for too short a period of time, as it will make you appear anxious.

- Be aware of non-verbal messages: listen with your ears, eyes, and heart. There are three aspects to conversation: verbal, visual, and vocal, and you need to take all of them into account to be able to fully understand the message the person is conveying. The verbal aspect is the words that people say. However, as well as listening to the words, also be aware of what else is happening, as this will form part of the message. The visual aspect comprises factors you can see, for example, facial expressions, gestures, and posture. The vocal aspect comprises factors you can hear, for example, intonation, speed, and volume. Notice if all three factors are congruent. A person's facial expressions and body language may support the verbal message, or may communicate a different message. Notice the "energy" the person gives off—if it is enthusiastic, resigned, bored, interested, and so on. Notice what is not said; listen for any emotions that may differ from the words people say. The better you get to know a person and the more you observe and analyze what they do, the better you will understand their particular way of communicating. Remember that a lot of communication is non-verbal. There is a Jewish proverb that says, "A mother understands what a child does not say."
- Understand the difference between a You-listener and an I-listener. You-listeners are focused on their conversation partner and are interested in hearing what the other person has to say. I-listeners are self-focused and aim to shape the conversation so they can talk about themselves. For example, if a You-Listener asks, "Where did you take the children yesterday?" and the other person responds with, "We went to the beach," the You-Listener will then show an interest in the other person and ask questions that relate to their answer, for example, "Which beach did you go to?" or "Did the children enjoy it?" However, if an I-Listener had asked the same question and received the same reply, their response would turn the attention back on themselves. For example, they may say, "Oh we went to the beach yesterday too. The weather was great and the children loved it. There's a special part of the beach we always go to and they spent hours ..." People like

to be listened to, so you will be seen as a more effective conversationalist if you develop the skills of a You-listener rather than an I-Listener.

A good question to ask yourself when it comes to the issue of listening is: Am I really listening, or am I just waiting for my turn to speak?

3. Speaking

As with listening skills, the skills for effective speaking also take time and practice to hone. Here are a few strategies you can use:

- Operate from a sense of being grounded. This ties in with feelings of confidence and self-worth. When you feel centered, you will speak in a way that attracts respect. For example, you will tend to talk more slowly and not rush to get your words out. You will avoid mumbling and will speak clearly and deliberately. You will also feel comfortable in holding eye contact with people. But which comes first, the feeling of being grounded or the way of behaving? Don't worry if you don't feel grounded yet, simply start practicing the behaviors of talking more slowly, enunciating clearly, and holding eye contact for around five seconds at a time, and your sense of feeling centered will grow.

- Present as a relaxed and at-ease person. It's common for people to pick up on the emotions of those around them, so if you appear nervous or ill-at-ease, others will start to feel ill-at-ease too. Fiddling with your hair, wiggling your foot, letting your sentences trail away, or constantly sounding unsure of yourself will make others feel uncomfortable. People generally prefer to feel relaxed and comfortable in conversation situations, so if you have a tendency to be ill-at-ease, it will be good to start making a few changes. Start off by simply noticing what behaviors you display that may be deemed as nervous behaviors. Then over a period of time, and in small steps, work on one behavior at a time, making slight improvements. For example, if you tend to fiddle with your hair, notice when you do it and simply stop and gently clasp your hands together or put them in your pockets. Over a period of time, it will become second nature not to fiddle with your hair.

- Make people feel good about themselves. People who bring out the best in other people tend to be well-liked, and tend to attract people to them. This is because the average person gives themselves many negative messages: "I'm too dumb," "I'm too old," "I'm too fat," "I'll never get promoted," "Nobody likes me" and such like, so that when someone else provides them with positive messages about themselves, they instantly warm to them. This doesn't mean we should give people empty compliments, it means we should make a point of noticing any positive aspects a person has, and bring them into the conversation from time to time.

- Avoid moaning, complaining, and speaking negatively on a regular basis. People generally prefer to be around positive, enthusiastic people, so the more enthusiasm you can genuinely show for a conversation topic—without becoming overly enthusiastic—the more people will enjoy talking to you. If it's a topic that doesn't totally capture your attention, still aim to find an aspect of it that you can show some enthusiasm for. It will certainly enhance your conversation skills!

- Include challenging comments and perceptions. It's said that the most engaging conversationalists are those who are the most challenging. They are people who make a point of being interested in, and finding out, about a wide range of topics so that they can have conversations with many people about many issues. They are also people who spend some time thinking about what they learn and working out their own viewpoint. It's fairly easy to repeat common views on ordinary topics, but effective conversationalists offer provocative insights.

- Avoid going off on tangents. It's OK to follow a new line of thought from time to time, but if your conversation is forever going off on tangents, it will be hard for people to follow what you are saying. One way to do this is to pause for two to three seconds before giving a response; during this time, work out roughly what your message is, and a couple of

points you could make along the way. If you become prac-
ticed at this, you can give focused responses and can avoid
rambling.

- Don't pretend to be perfect. People don't relate to perfection,
  it makes them feel inadequate. People like to hear—from time
  to time—humorous stories that are self-effacing and show you
  have a reasonable level of vulnerability. They like to hear something they can relate to that will make them say "Me too!" Be
  careful to use this technique wisely, however. Don't use it too
  much and avoid using it too early on when you meet someone
  new.

Conversations with grandchildren

Benefits of grandparent-grandchild conversation

For those children fortunate enough to have a grandparent who loves
them and wants to spend time with them, there are many benefits for
both the grandchild and the grandparent.

What are some of the things children say about having loving
grandparents in their lives? They say they are lucky because grandparents: like to be with them; have time to spend with them; give them
special treats; take them on outings; have time to walk slowly and
point out interesting things; don't say "hurry up"; spoil them a bit; read
the same story over and over again without missing any bits; answer
interesting questions like, "why is the sun yellow?" and "why do ducks
quack?"; kiss them even when they haven't been good; are really smart
and teach them lots of things. No doubt your grandchildren have said
something similar.

In addition, research has shown that:

- Grandparents can be invaluable for families with busy lives,
  where both parents work, or where there is a single parent.
  Grandparent involvement can help the parents and can
  fill a need in children's lives. Sometimes a grandparent can
  reach out to a child when a parent can't. Sometimes grandchildren will only share something of importance with a
  grandparent.

- When parents separate or when there are family changes, grandparents can be there as a listening ear and a support.
- Youngsters who spend time with grandparents generally cope better socially and have fewer behavioral problems. The fact that there is a grandparent around who cares about them can make a huge difference in the children's lives.
- The relationship and type of love a grandchild has with a grandparent is one that can't be obtained elsewhere, it's a much easier and less complicated type of love than a child can have with his or her parents. It makes them feel special, a kind of special they know they won't get from anyone else.
- The grandparent-grandchild relationship gives children a sense of their history and heritage and where they fit into the world.
- As grandparents are younger and more active nowadays, and many are online and more aware of issues in the world of their grandchildren, this helps build good relationships. Being younger, they may even share some hobbies and interests, which gives the opportunity for conversation, bonding, and fun times.
- Ordinary day-to-day activities can provide the opportunity for grandparents to teach new things and new vocabulary to their grandchildren. A trip to the supermarket, for example, brings the chance to show them new foods, teach the names of vegetables, discuss prices, talk about where foods come from, examine different types of packaging, do some counting and addition, and much more.

There are many benefits for the grandparents in the relationship too. For example:

- There is less pressure being a grandparent than a parent.
- If you made some mistakes as a parent you can have a go at getting it right this time.
- It gives you a younger outlook and you can indulge yourself in the things you'd like to do, but can't without a young child, like buy games, watch cartoons, play in the snow, or go on the swings. You get to bring the magic of Santa back into your life as well.

- You can see the world through the eyes of a child and feel their sense of wonder and joy. Everything becomes new and exciting again.
- You can have fun times with them and then "give them back" to their parents—so you get a lot of joy with few downsides.
- Your grandchildren can teach you a lot about the world of today, especially about technology.

Spending quality time with your grandchildren and having wholesome conversations with them can produce more benefits than you may have imagined:

- For example, it's said that if a child doesn't have face-to-face conversations with responsive adults they will not learn to communicate properly. They learn through the feedback they gain from two-way interactions. Watching TV, for example, is a one-way interaction.
- Do you provide a suitable "Yes" environment? If a child is in a "No" environment—an environment where an adult is always saying "No" to a conversation with them, "No" to answering their questions, "No" to new experiences, "No" to risk taking and so on—the child will develop little interest in the world and the experiences it offers. They may become bored easily because there is only a small range of activities that interest them.
- If a child asks questions and is not answered, or is told that their questions are dumb, or is told off for constantly asking, then they will stop asking questions, will become indifferent, and will learn much less than they are capable of. It may seem challenging to answer all the questions a young child throws at you, but it is an integral and important part of the learning process for them.
- If a child is ridiculed for the things they say or ask, they will learn to keep their thoughts to themselves. In the words of the poet Henry Wadsworth Longfellow, "A torn jacket is soon mended; but hard words bruise the heart of a child." A supportive environment can do wonders for children's self-worth.

- Story telling offers more than just fun and bonding. If a child is not told stories or doesn't have stories read to them, they will see little reason for developing an interest in the world of books. Einstein believed that telling and reading stories was a basis for increasing a child's intelligence.

- If children are asked questions and are encouraged to give thoughtful answers, it helps them learn to think for themselves and not simply take on board the thinking of others. It helps them solve problems and come up with ways of reasoning and behaving that are well thought-out and appropriate for their own needs. It lays the foundations for adulthood, for when the questions become harder.

There are many unseen advantages for spending time talking with your grandchildren, and the time you invest will be of enormous benefit both to them and to you.

Communicating with children

Some aspects of conversation are the same, whether we are talking with children or adults. For example, being a good listener and understanding the concept of turn taking are important no matter who we are speaking to.

Some aspects, however, are different when we are in conversation with children. During the time that children are developing their conversation skills, their way of communicating may differ from that of an adult. They have different ways of seeing the world; they have different ways of expressing themselves; there are some concepts they have yet to encounter; they may not have the words to express what they are feeling; and they are in the process of learning society's "rules" for conversation.

It's useful, therefore, to be aware that you may have to adapt your way of communicating. Listed below are a few of the issues to bear in mind.

Start early

You can start building a relationship with your grandchild even before they acquire language. Simply being with them and talking to them helps them get used to you being there; to your voice and to a level of relationship with you. Even when they can only make babbling noises, respond as if it were language. Talking and listening to children from as young an age as possible will start to form communication habits that will help when they are older.

As your grandchildren become teenagers, there may be fewer opportunities to have conversations with them—they may spend more time with friends, or may go through a phase of talking very little. However, if you've built as strong a relationship as possible when they were younger, the bonds will still be there when they come back to the stage of being able to have more conversations with you.

Younger children

During the early years of language acquisition, the words you utter will form only part of a child's way of making sense of what you say. They will still need to take account of your facial expressions, your gestures, and your tone of voice. Remember that the words on their own may not adequately convey your message.

Explain why

When you are giving instructions or explanations, note that younger children need an understanding of cause and effect, and why we should or shouldn't do things.

For example, instead of just saying, "Close the door," there are times when it's useful to give a brief explanation: "If you leave the door open the heat will leave the room and we'll get cold. Please close the door."

Open vs. closed questions

With children, we need to use more open questions than closed questions. Closed questions tend to lead to one-word answers. For example, the question, "Do you like to watch TV?" will probably produce a "Yes" or "No" answer. Open questions tend to lead to longer answers and are usually better for keeping the conversation flowing; for example, "What kind of TV programs do you like to watch?"

Younger children have the tendency to take closed questions literally and therefore give short answers, while older children have learned that you can give open answers to closed questions to keep the conversation going. For example, if you ask them, "Do you like to watch TV?" an older child may answer along the lines of, "I watch the cartoons when I come home from school..."

A useful open-question phrase you can use is, "Tell me about...." If you were looking at one of their drawings, for example, instead of saying, "What's that a drawing of?" you could say, "Tell me about your drawing."

Aim to avoid making an open question too vague. For example, if you asked your grandchild, "Do you like school?" and they replied "Yes." And then you said, "Tell me more," this may be too open a question for them. Instead ask questions about specific aspects of school, such as, "Tell me about your teacher, what is she like?", "Tell me what happens when you go into your classroom in the mornings."

Very broad questions, such as, "What are you thinking about?" will probably produce replies such as "Nothing" or "I dunno." A more specific question, such as, "Which of these jigsaws do you want to do?" will be an easier question for them to deal with.

Be careful when using the words "Why?" or "Why not?" In some circumstances they can sound confrontational and may make the child feel defensive. For example, if a child says, "I don't want to go to school," instead of responding with "Why not?" there may be a softer way to ask the question, such as, "Tell me what's been happening there" or "What's making you unhappy?"

There may be times when a closed question, or a question where you give specific options, may make the child give an answer that isn't accurate, simply because they feel obliged to answer your question. For example, if you were to ask, "What do you think about X, do you love it or hate it?" they may not feel either of these emotions towards it, but may choose one of the options just to please you.

You can also explain to your grandchild that if they don't know the answer to something you ask them, it's OK to say "I don't know"; and if they don't want to answer one of your questions, that's OK too.

Quantity and time

Be aware that younger children may have difficulty with quantity and time. If you ask them, "How many people were at the show?" they may give an answer such as, "There were a hundred, or maybe six, or maybe forty seven." Their ability to deal with quantities may not be developed yet.

Similarly with time; if you ask them how long ago something happened, or what time they start school in the morning, or how long until they go on vacation, these may be difficult concepts for them.

Use your grandchild's name

To enhance the conversation, use their name from time to time, though not too much as it will feel unnatural: "So, Rachel, if you had a magic carpet where would you go?"

Listen

Children especially need to be listened to, as it builds their feelings of self-worth and shows that what they are saying is valued by others. It makes them feel special, and helps build a confidence that will stand them in good stead for their future.

If they know you will listen without judging, they are more likely to be open to talking about sensitive issues, which can help them make sense of the world they are coming to grips with.

Being able to listen can also help you appreciate the child's level of understanding about issues. For example, if they ask, "What is X?", before you launch into an answer, you can check their level of knowledge by asking, "What do you know about X already?"

Show you are listening

How will they know you are listening? Asking questions is a good way to demonstrate this. It shows you are taking in what they are saying and are interested enough to find out more. Be careful about interrupting in order to ask questions, though. Give them enough time to say what they want to say before you jump in and ask a question.

Another way is to reflect back what they have said to show you are listening: for example, "Gosh, you got four presents from Santa?" "So 'Half Magic' is your favorite book?" "You were a bit sad yesterday?"

With young children you can also say things like "Wow!" "Really?" "Then what happened?" to show you are interested. But don't overdo the enthusiasm!

Feelings and emotions

Be open to listening when your grandchild has strong feelings or emotions. Avoid trying to deny or minimize their feelings, by saying, for example, "Oh you don't need to get upset about that," "I'm sure you don't really hate school," or "Being angry won't help."

It's useful for children to learn that it's OK to talk about how they are feeling and that someone will listen with love and understanding and will not judge them. Let them express their emotion, accept what they say, probe a little, and talk it through.

If they don't know how to express what they are feeling, try reflecting back to them what they have said and check if it's what they wanted to get across.

It may also be helpful to let them know that expressing emotion is OK if done in the right manner, and then to show them how to express it in an acceptable way. For example, letting people know that you are angry is different from being angry.

Awkward questions

Most children want to know about issues that may be difficult to talk about, for example, death, illness, drugs, sex, or abuse. Usually it's their parents they will discuss these with, but they may also turn to you.

If they specifically want to talk to you, it's important to create the right kind of atmosphere so that your grandchild feels they are able to discuss any topic without fear of negative consequences.

If they ask an awkward question, please don't aim to avoid answering—"I don't know, shall we watch TV?"—instead see it as an opportunity to help them learn about the bigger issues in the world in a compassionate and rational way.

You don't need to answer there and then if the situation isn't appropriate; you can suggest that you talk about it when you get home, for example. This will also give you some thinking time. If you don't know the answer, you could suggest that you both look it up together. Be aware that children will find out one way or another, and it's better they find out an accurate answer from you.

An additional benefit for talking about bigger issues is that it gives you the opportunity to share (not impose) your values and ethics with your grandchild.

Be honest

Children need you to be honest so they can learn to trust and build a strong relationship. There is a difference between telling a white lie to protect a child's innocence—for example, the concept of Santa or the Tooth Fairy—and not being honest; and most parents and grandparents have a gut feeling as to where the boundary is.

While there may be certain times where it's not appropriate for children to know all the details, telling them untruths can ultimately be more harmful.

If we don't give a suitable answer, they may devise their own explanation, which may be scarier and more upsetting to them than the real answer.

Give them time

Sometimes children take a long time to work out and vocalize what they want to say. Resist the temptation to finish off what they are saying or to jump in and ask questions in order to hurry them up. Respect their need to take time; give them the space to say what they want to at their own pace, even when they speak slowly and have lots of gaps.

If they are always hurried, they may think that they need to speak quickly because what they say is of little value and needs to take up as small amount of other people's time as possible. Patience pays dividends!

Types of questions

There are several types of questions that crop up in conversation. These include questions for clarification, and questions to help the conversation continue.

For example, if your grandchild says, "We went to the park today and played on the swings," a clarification question may be to find out who the "we" refers to, so you may ask, "Who did you go to the park with?"

Or, if your grandchild says, "I like going to the park with you," a question to help the conversation continue may be, "So when we go next time, what shall we do?"

The talkative continuum

When my brother and I were teenagers, my mother would ask us, after we got home from school, what had happened during our day. My brother would then proceed to relate every detail from the moment he left the house in the morning until the moment he arrived home. When it was my turn to reply I would simply say "Nothing." Exasperated, my mother would exclaim, "Kim, you think you should tell me something only if it's of earth-shattering importance!" To which I would calmly reply "Yes."

And it was true; I really didn't see any need to relate what I saw as very ordinary events that varied little from day to day and week to week: I went to school, I did some lessons, and I came home again. Events of earth-shattering importance rarely happened.

Nowadays my mother finds it amusing that I became a conference speaker and a trainer in communication skills. "Were you saving up all your words until you became an adult?" she asks. Furthermore, my daughter is now a teenager, and when I ask her, "What happened at school today?" she always replies "Nothing." I find myself saying, "But *something* must have happened" until I realise she is going through the same stage that I went through.

All children, and in fact all people, fall somewhere on a "talkative" continuum. Some are at the extremely talkative end of the continuum and rarely stop for breath, some are at the other end and say very little, while most fall somewhere in the middle. Some will want to tell you about every aspect of a particular issue, while others will see little point in speaking unless there is an issue of great magnitude to discuss. Not every grandchild likes to talk; some are introverted and prefer to live in the world of their own thoughts, while some are extroverted and love to have an audience who will listen to everything they say.

People's place on the continuum can vary from time to time depending on how they are feeling, who they are with, the situation they are in, or perhaps their age. Sometimes their level of talkativeness may be affected by lack of confidence, too much confidence, stressful situations, the conversation topic, or talking with someone who either helps or hinders conversation.

Understanding this and respecting where people are on the continuum can make for more satisfying conversations. Those who try to make people more talkative than they naturally are, or than they want to be in a particular situation, may find this works against what they are trying to achieve.

Silence

Silence is a natural, and oftentimes useful, part of conversation. It's OK to have silence from time to time and there is no need to fill all the gaps.

Some people can formulate and deliver a response very quickly, while others may take some time to think up their reply. If you leave enough space for the people who take time, they will be able to respond appropriately.

There are instances when it's useful to leave a comfortable silence for a period of time to give the other person the opportunity to open up if they want to. They may need to build up their confidence to share something with you; they may need time to process what they want to say; or they may need to know that if they share something significant, that you will allow them the space to speak at their own pace and not feel the need to jump in and fill all the silences. They may also need to know that you will have a respect for what they say and will not judge them. If you have a feeling that they may want to share something, be aware that it may take a few times of being with you before they feel able to open up.

Sometimes children choose to be silent. Don't worry (they don't hate you!), for the most part this is OK; they may have little to say or may be simply coping with the changes that occur as part of growing up.

Be prepared

A while ago I met a woman who was in her forties, single, and without children. She had teenage nephews and nieces she saw infrequently. However, she was interested enough in her nephews and nieces to research their "world" and find out the kinds of things they were interested in and would like to talk about.

"Can you have conversations with them?" I asked.

"Oh yes," she replied, "I can speak 'teenager.'"

To have the best conversations you can with your grandchild, find out about things they like so that you can talk about them. What are their interests? Do they like particular toys, TV programs, sports, books, celebrities, or film characters? Learn about them. Do they like to play particular games? Do you fancy learning how to play them? Give yourself a head start, the conversation may flow more easily and they'll think you're a pretty cool grandparent!

Cultivate conversation times

You may like to create special times when the two of you are together doing a task that no one else does so you can have a conversation. Make it into a pleasant ritual. An activity where the child feels their contribution is helpful and valued will make them feel special and more likely to communicate.

For example, can you both do the washing up together; can you go into the garden and do some gardening for a while; can you go fishing together; can you do some baking together; can they help you sort out the spare room; can you look through photograph albums together?

Special moments of conversation can often happen when you are engaged in an activity together.

Alternatively, if your grandchild is happy to just talk with you, make the opportunity to sit down for a while and have a chat. It's nice to have a break from activities and sit down together with nothing else to do apart from talk.

Use language children can understand

It's easy to forget that adults use words and sentence structures that children may find difficult to understand, so it's useful to have an awareness of the language you use when you are with your grandchildren.

For example, do you use complex sentence structures; long or difficult words; words that children may not be familiar with; acronyms or jargon; or things such as idioms, for example, "Don't count your chickens before they hatch"? While these may be a regular part of your conversation, children may not be at this level yet.

Short sentences with short words are a good rule of thumb for younger children. If you are explaining something or giving instructions, split it up into small, easily digestible chunks, making them as straightforward as possible. If your grandchild's attention starts to wander, it means they no longer understand or are no longer interested.

Quick tip: A way to build your skills is to listen to how children communicate with each other and see what you notice.

Use age-appropriate language

As children grow up, the level of language they understand increases, so be careful not to use "baby" language or language that is too "young" for older children. This is something to be especially aware of when you don't see your grandchildren on a regular basis, and you may forget they will have changed since you last saw them.

If you are talking with children of different ages, they are likely to be at different developmental levels, and you may need to use different language or give different information to them.

For sensitive or important information, you may need to explain it to, or talk it through with, the children separately at a level that is appropriate for each child. Talking about divorce, health issues and death for example with children of different ages would be difficult and may not allow them to ask the questions they need to ask.

Repetition

Most people learn through repetition; the more we hear something, the more likely we are to understand and remember it.

Younger children particularly like to have repetition, and so they may ask you the same question more than once, or want you to tell the same story more than once, or want to talk about the same thing more than once.

Repetition is normal; it's all part of the learning process, so be prepared for it and be prepared to be tolerant!

For your part, if you want to give information or instructions to your grandchild, using repetition is useful. Repeating the message in another way will help them understand.

Remaining calm

Parents and grandparents who can remain calm, restrained, and tolerant will keep the door to communication open. They will be the ones whose children and grandchildren keep talking to them, no matter the issue at hand, because the child knows that they will be treated with a level of respect.

If a child is agitated, or if you are feeling irritated, and the conversation becomes heated, the child will learn keep quiet in the future in order to avoid similar potential conflict situations.

1000 QUESTIONS AND CONVERSATION STARTERS

The starters fall into five separate sections, in total comprising 100 different topic areas, each containing ten questions or conversation starters:

SECTION 1
For grandchildren to ask their grandparents

When You Were Born
Your Family
Childhood (1)
Childhood (2)
School
Your Teenage Years
Becoming an Adult
Marriage
Becoming a Parent
My Mom
My Dad
My Granddad
My Grandma
Favorites

About Me
Let's Compare!
Choices
Like You
What Do You Think?
Exciting Adventures
Advice
Friends
Getting Older
Your Thoughts (1)
Your Thoughts (2)
Being Rude
Your Call!

SECTION 2
For grandparents to ask their grandchildren

School and High School   Creative Questions
Favorites   Your Future
Home and Interests   Teenagers
Good Things   ... In the World
Silly Questions   Activities
Growing Up   Let's Pretend
This and That   Discussion Topics
Your Family: grandparents   What Would You Do If?
Your Family: Mom   Fun!
Your Family: Dad   This and That
Fun Questions   Magic Wand
Tell a Story   Scenarios (1) for younger
Joint Stories (1)   children
Joint Stories (2)   Scenarios (2) for teenagers
Thinking   Your Call!

SECTION 3
For grandparents to ask their children

Being a Parent
Parenting, Grandparenting, and Family

SECTION 4
For grandparent couples to ask each other

Early Days   Our Grandchildren
About You and Me (1)   The Future
About You and Me (2)   Would You Like...?
About You and Me (3)   Music
Family   Who Is...?
Grandparenting (1)   Parenting and
Grandparenting (2)   Grandparenting
Our Children

SECTION 5

For grandparents in general conversation

Being a Grandparent (1)

Being a Grandparent (2)

Being a Grandparent (3)

Grandparent Views (1)

Grandparent Views (2)

Your Predictions

The Things Grandchildren Say

Then and Now

What Would You Do?

Stereotypes

Protecting Grandchildren

Challenging Issues (1)

Challenging Issues (2)

1–10

Spending Time with Grandchildren

Marriage

Aging

Those Special Things

Advice Column (1)

Advice Column (2)

Advice Column (3)

Lessons

Travel

Money

Work and Business

Fun!

Males and Females

Reading

Plus ... Your Favorites & Your Starters

SECTION 1

For grandchildren to ask their grandparents

When You Were Born

- What do you know about your birth?
- Where were you born?
- How did your parents choose your name?
- Who else was in your family when you were born?
- Did anyone buy you a teddy bear?

(GPCH) If I had known how wonderful it would be to have grandchildren, I'd have had them first. *Lois Wyse, advertising executive, author, and columnist.*

- Have you got any photos of when you were a baby?
- What kinds of clothes did you wear when you were a baby?
- Do you know what your pram was like?
- Did you have any health problems when you were a baby?
- What was happening in the world when you were born?

(GPCH) Grandchildren are the dots that connect the lines from generation to generation. *Lois Wyse, advertising executive, author, and columnist.*

Your Family

- What are your mom and dad's names?
- How did your mom and dad meet?
- What work did your mom and dad do?
- Were your parents strict with you?
- What do you remember most about your parents when you were growing up?

> **(GPCH)** Grandmas are moms with lots of frosting. *Author Unknown.*

- How many brothers and sisters do you have and are they older or younger than you?
- How did you get on with your brothers and sisters when you were a child?
- What were your grandparents like?
- What other family members did you spend a lot of time with?
- Which family member made you laugh the most?

> **(GPCH)** If nothing is going well, call your grandmother. *Italian Proverb.*

Childhood (1)

- What is the earliest thing you remember?
- What was your bedroom like?
- Will you tell me about some of your toys?
- Was there any food you used to hate?
- Do you remember any birthday presents people gave you?

> **(GPCH)** Children need love, especially when they do not deserve it. *Harold Hulbert, American psychiatrist.*

- What was your best family vacation?
- Were there things that made you unhappy when you were a child?

- What's the best thing that happened to you when you were a child?
- What did you used to get into trouble for?
- Did you have to do any household chores?

> **(GPCH)** A three year old child is a being who gets almost as much fun out of a fifty-six dollar set of swings as it does out of finding a small green worm. *Bill Vaughan, columnist and author.*

Childhood (2)

- What did you do at the weekends?
- Did you have a heartthrob?
- Do you remember the address of the house you grew up in and what it was like?
- Did you have a garden?
- What was your neighborhood like?

> **(GPCH)** Grandchildren: the only people who can get more out of you than the IRS. *Gene Perret, comedy writer.*

- Did you have a nickname?
- Did you have a favorite book?
- Did you have a pet?
- What games did you play with your friends?
- Was it safe to play in the streets?

> **(GPCH)** The reason grandparents and grandchildren get along so well is that they have a common enemy. *Sam Levenson, humorist, writer, teacher, and television host.*

School

- What was your first school like?
- What is the earliest thing you remember about school?
- Did you like school?

- Can you remember your first teacher?
- What was the classroom and playground like at your school?

(GPCH) It's interesting that I had such a close relationship with my grandfather. Because your parents always judge you: they say, "You shouldn't do this, you shouldn't do that." But with your grandparents you have a feeling that you can say anything or you can do anything, and they will support you. That's why you have this kind of connection. *Novak Djokovic, professional tennis player.*

- What happened in the school playground?
- Did you like doing sports at school?
- What did you wear to school?
- What were your best and worst subjects?
- Did you find it easy to learn to read and write?

(GPCH) Nobody can do for little children what grandparents do. Grandparents sort of sprinkle stardust over the lives of little children. *Alex Haley, author.*

Your Teenage Years

- What was it like being a teenager?
- What was the best part about being a teenager?
- What was the hardest part about being a teenager?
- Did you have a boyfriend or girlfriend?
- Did people get married when they were teenagers?

(GPCH) A characteristic of the normal child is he doesn't act that way very often. *Author Unknown.*

- Who were the popular singers and bands when you were a teenager?
- Who were the popular film stars when you were a teenager?
- What did teenagers do for fun?
- What events happened in the world when you were in your teens?
- What kinds of clothes and shoes did teenagers wear?

(GPCH) Children make your life important. *Erma Bombeck, humorist and author.*

Becoming an Adult

- When do you think you became an adult?
- Did you do anything to show you were an adult, such as wearing certain clothes, using make-up, or drinking alcohol?
- When did you leave home?
- What was your first house like?
- When did you get your first job and what did you do?

(GPCH) I enjoyed my grandparents very much. My mother and father would always allow me to stay with them. *Dominic Chianese, film, television, and theatre actor.*

- Did your parents still treat you like a child when you had grown up?
- Was it easy to get jobs back then?
- Did you have a bank account?
- Was it normal for people to learn to drive, and have a car?
- What was your hairstyle like?

(GPCH) I was raised by my grandparents, and they always made sure that I had a pencil and some paper, whether we were in the car or at a restaurant. While they were enjoying a nice meal, I would be sitting there drawing funny pictures of the waitress. *Jarrett J. Krosoczka, author and illustrator.*

Marriage

- How did you meet the person you married?
- What did you like about them?
- How did they propose to you, or how did you propose to them?
- Will you tell me about the wedding ceremony and celebrations?
- What were people's wedding outfits like?

> **(GPCH)** I'm really confident. I had a perfect childhood. I had perfect parents and grandparents. They just love me, simply. So I have no fears. *Melanie Laurent, actress, model, director, singer, and writer.*

- How much did your wedding cost?
- Did you go on honeymoon?
- Do you still have wedding photos? What are they like?
- If you could go back and change one thing about your wedding, what would you change?
- Did you have a house when you got married?

> **(GPCH)** I'm raising my daughter with her grandparents in the picture, and that feels good. *Paula Cole, singer-songwriter.*

Becoming a Parent

- Did your mom and dad give you advice about becoming a parent?
- What was it like having a new baby? Did you know how to look after a baby?
- How did you choose your children's names?
- Were most women stay-at-home moms?
- What did you love most about your children when they were little?

> **(GPCH)** I think the great thing about grandparents is seeing another home, realizing that people you love can have different priorities, different diversions, different opinions, and lead quite different lives from the ones you see every day, and that is immensely valuable. *Simon Hoggart, English journalist and broadcaster.*

- What trouble did your children get into?
- Am I like them?
- Tell me about a funny incident that happened with your children.

- What did you do for special events like Christmas or Thanksgiving?
- What's the difference between having a child and having a grandchild?

> **(GPCH)** If you haven't time to respond to a tug at your pants leg, your schedule is too crowded. *Robert Brault, writer.*

My Mom

- What was my mom like when she was a baby?
- What was my mom's favorite toy?
- What was my mom like when she was at school?
- Tell me something funny that my mom did when she was little.
- What was the naughtiest thing my mom did?

> **(GPCH)** I have three grandchildren and am hoping for twenty. *Maureen Forrester, Canadian opera singer.*

- What was my mom interested in when she was a girl?
- What were my mom's friends like?
- What was my mom like when she became a teenager?
- What did my mom want to be when she grew up?
- Did my mom keep her bedroom tidy?

> **(GPCH)** A grandfather is someone with silver in his hair and gold in his heart. *Author Unknown.*

My Dad

- What was my dad like when he was a boy?
- Did my dad have a teddy bear when he was little?
- Did my dad like going to school?
- What did my dad want to be when he grew up?
- Did my dad like to do boys' things?

(GPCH) The simplest toy, one which even the youngest child can operate, is called a grandparent. *Sam Levenson, humorist, writer, teacher, and television host.*

- What did my dad keep in his bedroom?
- What things made my dad laugh when he was a kid?
- What were my dad's friends like?
- What did the two of you used to do together?
- What was my dad good at?

(GPCH) Children seldom misquote. In fact, they usually repeat word for word what you shouldn't have said. *Author Unknown.*

My Granddad

Questions to ask grandma about granddad (please change the names "granddad" and "grandma" to whatever names your grandchild uses):

- What did granddad look like when you first met him?
- Is granddad different now than when you first met him?
- Does granddad have any funny habits?
- What does granddad do that makes you laugh?
- What's the best "granddad" thing he does?

(GPCH) Grandfathers are for loving and fixing things. *Author Unknown.*

- Does granddad do anything silly?
- What can I do that will make granddad laugh?
- Have you and granddad ever had a special name for each other?
- Does granddad like to have adventures?
- Tell me about something brave that granddad did.

(GPCH) Grandchildren don't stay young forever, which is good because Pop-pops have only so many horsey rides in them. *Gene Perret, comedy writer.*

My Grandma

Questions to ask granddad about grandma (please change the names "granddad" and "grandma" to whatever names your grandchild uses):

- What did grandma look like when you first met her?
- Is grandma different now than when you first met her?
- What is grandma really good at?
- What things make grandma laugh?
- Is grandma afraid of anything?

(GPCH) Grandma always made you feel she had been waiting to see just you all day and now the day was complete. *Marcy DeMaree, author.*

- Where is grandma's favorite place?
- What is grandma's favorite food?
- What can I do to make grandma happy?
- Does grandma like to sing or dance?
- Does grandma have any funny habits?

(GPCH) Grandmas never run out of hugs or cookies. *Author Unknown.*

Favorites

- What is your favorite food?
- What is your favorite color?
- What is your favorite time of the day?
- What is your favorite animal?
- What is your favorite memory?

(GPCH) I continue to believe that if children are given the necessary tools to succeed, they will succeed beyond their wildest dreams! *David Vitter, U.S. senator.*

- What was your favorite activity when you were growing up?
- Who was your favorite teacher when you were at school?
- Where is your favorite place?

- What is your favorite flavor of ice cream?
- What is your favorite store?

> **(GPCH)** Only where children gather is there any real chance of fun. *Mignon McLaughlin, journalist and author.*

About Me

- What did you say when you found out I'd been born?
- What was I like when I was born?
- Did I do anything cute when I was little?
- Did I do anything naughty when I was little?
- What do you think I'll be when I grow up?

> **(GPCH)** Hugs can do great amounts of good, especially for children. *Princess Diana, Princess of Wales.*

- What's the thing I'm best at?
- Who do I most look like?
- What always makes me laugh?
- What things do you and I have in common?
- If you could go on an adventure with me, where would you like to go and what would you like to do?

> **(GPCH)** The most interesting information comes from children, for they tell all they know and then stop. *Mark Twain, American author and humorist.*

Let's Compare!

Let's see if our childhoods are similar or different:

- This is what my classroom looks like .... What did yours look like?
- This is what I take to school with me .... What did you used to take to school?

- These are the names of the children in my class .... What were the names of the children you can remember?
- These are my favorite clothes .... What were your favorite clothes?
- These are my heroes .... Who were your heroes?

> **(GPCH)** A child can ask questions that a wise man cannot answer. *Author Unknown.*

- These are the treats I like to have .... What treats did you used to have?
- This is how much pocket money I get .... How much pocket money did you get?
- These are the places I go with my family for a day out .... Did you used to go for days out with your family?
- This is the time I go to bed .... What time did you go to bed when you were my age?
- These are the songs I like .... What songs did you like?

> **(GPCH)** A grandmother is a little bit parent, a little bit teacher, and a little bit best friend. *Author Unknown.*

Choices

See what your grandchildren can discover about you when they ask which of these choices you will opt for. Which will you choose? You have to make a choice and give your reasons:

- Would you rather
    - have a lie-in, eat breakfast in bed, and read the paper/watch television, then get taken out to do some sightseeing
    - or get up early, do some exercise, have breakfast in a café, then go on an adventure trek with a group of people?

- Would you rather
  - spend a day at the zoo learning about being a zookeeper
  - or spend a day at an art course learning a new type of art or craft?
- Would you rather
  - have an evening out at the opera
  - or go ten pin-bowling?
- If you were given $1000 would you rather
  - buy something for the house or garden
  - or buy items to wear?
- Would you rather
  - take part in a TV quiz show
  - or be interviewed on the radio about an issue in your community?

(GPCH) Most grandmas have a touch of the scallywag. *Helen Thomson, actress.*

- You have been entered for the Best Grandparent award. Which category would you like to be in:
  - the funniest grandparent
  - the silliest grandparent
  - the noisiest grandparent
  - the cheekiest grandparent
  - the fastest grandparent
  - the sleepiest grandparent
  - the best cook
  - the best gardener
  - the best storyteller
  - the best mender of broken items
  - the best babysitter
  - the best adventurer
  - the best educator
  - the best listener
  - or something else?
- If you had to do something exciting would you rather:
  - travel into space with the new galactic spaceships
  - go on safari to East Africa to see the gorillas

- ○ go on an expedition to the Antarctic
- ○ spend a month helping to build an orphanage in India
- ○ or present an award on television to a famous person?
- Would you rather
  - ○ spend a day somewhere very, very cold
  - ○ or spend a day somewhere very, very hot?
- If you could go back to a time before you were born and change a world event from history, what would you change?
- If you could spend a day with a famous person, who would you spend it with and what would you like to do?

(GPCH) Grandmas hold our tiny hands for just a little while, but our hearts forever. *Author Unknown.*

Like You

- Which one of your family looks most like you?
- Which cartoon character is most like you?
- Is there a famous person who looks a bit like you?
- Which type of dog looks most like you?
- Do I look like you at all?

(GPCH) Our grandchildren accept us for ourselves, without rebuke or effort to change us, as no one in our entire lives has ever done, not our parents, siblings, spouses, friends—and hardly ever our own grown children. *Ruth Goode, author.*

- Will I look like you when I am your age?
- Who do you know who has the same hobbies as you?
- Do you know anyone who likes the same kind of music or books or movies as you?
- Who do you know who laughs at the same things as you do?
- What skill could you teach me so I can learn to be as good as you?

(GPCH) Tell the children the truth. *Bob Marley, singer-songwriter.*

What Do You Think?

- Do you think there are aliens on other planets?
- Do you think it's good to have lots and lots of money?
- Do you think ghosts live in haunted houses?
- Do you believe in God?
- What do you think happens when we die?

> **(GPCH)** There's nothing that can help you understand your beliefs more than trying to explain them to an inquisitive child. *Frank A. Clark, American politician.*

- Who do you think should be the president or leader of our country?
- Do you think it's OK to eat food like burgers and fries?
- What time do you think children should go to bed at night?
- Do you think we should give money to poor people in other countries?
- How do you think children should help their mom and dad around the house?

> **(GPCH)** Children are educated by what the grown-up is and not by his talk. *Carl Jung, Swiss psychiatrist and psychotherapist.*

Exciting Adventures

- Tell me about the most exciting adventure you've ever had.
- Do you have to be really brave to go on an adventure?
- Has my mom or dad ever been on an adventure?
- If you could be a famous adventurer, who would you like to be?
- What is the best adventure story you've ever read?

> **(GPCH)** I love music of all kinds, but there's no greater music than the sound of my grandchildren laughing; my kids, too. *Sylvia Earle, oceanographer, explorer, author, and lecturer.*

- Tell me about an adventure that someone you know has been on.
- Do you think we could go to the center of the earth?
- If we were astronauts and went into space, what kinds of aliens would we meet?
- If we met a genie who gave us a magic lamp and told us to make a wish, what should we wish for?
- If a big, flying dragon came to the house and said it would take us on an adventure, should we go to caves in the mountains or an island with a volcano?

> **(GPCH)** You know the only people who are always sure about the proper way to raise children? Those who've never had any. *Bill Cosby, comedian, actor, and author.*

Advice

Questions for teenagers and older grandchildren to ask:

- What advice would you give to teenagers these days?
- Are qualifications the most important way to create a good future?
- What kind of work do you think I'm best suited to?
- What do you wish you had known when you were my age?
- What advice can you give me about choosing a husband, wife or partner?

> **(GPCH)** How true Daddy's words were when he said: all children must look after their own upbringing. Parents can only give good advice or put them on the right paths, but the final forming of a person's character lies in their own hands. *Anne Frank, writer and Jewish victim of the Holocaust.*

- What's the easiest way to learn about politics?
- What's your definition of success?
- What advice can you give me about money?
- What are some good lifelong habits to adopt?
- Is there anything I should be working on now to prepare for my future?

(GPCH) I really wanted to retire and rest and spend more time with my children, my grandchildren, and of course with my wife. *Nelson Mandela, South African anti-apartheid revolutionary, politician, and philanthropist.*

Friends

- Will you tell me about the friends you had at school?
- Who was your best friend when you were a child?
- Did you and your friends get into trouble?
- Did you ever fall out with your friends?
- Who was the best man or chief bridesmaid at your wedding and why did you choose them?

(GPCH) On the seventh day God rested. His grandchildren must have been out of town. *Gene Perret, comedy writer.*

- Who is your best friend now?
- What do you like doing with your friends now?
- Is it OK if people don't have a best friend?
- What advice can you give about friendships?
- What should people do if they fall out with one of their friends?

(GPCH) You can learn many things from children. How much patience you have, for instance. *Franklin P. Jones, reporter, public relations executive, and humorist.*

Getting Older

- What were you like when you were my age?
- Do you think you are old?
- How old do you feel?
- What's the best thing about getting older?
- What's the worst thing about getting older?

(GPCH) Perfect love sometimes does not come until the first grandchild. *Welsh Proverb.*

- Are you worried about old age?
- What things do you do to keep yourself young?
- What can you do now, that you couldn't do when you were younger?
- Which movie stars are about the same age as you?
- If you could choose to be a certain age forever, what age would you choose?

(GPCH) The greatest gifts you can give your children are the roots of responsibility and the wings of independence. *Denis Waitley, author.*

Your Thoughts (1)

I'll read out these items and you have to say what you think about them:
- Going to the beach
- Eating vegetables
- Traveling long distance in the car
- Riding a bike
- Going to a fancy dress party

(GPCH) Do you know why grandchildren are always so full of energy? They suck it out of their grandparents. *Gene Perret, comedy writer.*

- Staying in a posh hotel
- Beauty pageants for children
- Skateboarding
- Reading in bed
- Wearing glasses

(GPCH) I have two grandchildren. I want to hand them a planet and community that is really thriving. *Donald Berwick, American public servant.*

Your Thoughts (2)

I'll read out these items and you have to say what you think about them:
- Having homework to do
- Getting a tattoo

- Eating snails, and frogs' legs
- Being a grandparent
- Feeling really, really bored

> **(GPCH)** My real achievement is my daughter and my three beautiful grandchildren. *Marilyn Horne, opera singer.*

- Having gray hair
- Getting married
- Forgetting where you left your keys
- Staying in bed when you aren't feeling well
- Christmas

> **(GPCH)** Grandchildren have taught me how important the future is. I try to look through their eyes and envision what's in their imagination. What's the world going to look like when they're my age? That really does take a huge imagination. *Richard Lugar, American politician.*

Being Rude

- Do you burp?
- Does your tummy make a noise?
- Is it OK to say rude words?
- Were you ever rude to your parents?
- If a teacher asks a child to do something and they say "No," what should the teacher do?

> **(GPCH)** When my twin grandchildren were born two years ago, it changed me. I felt it was the essence of what life is about, and I cried all day. *André Rieu, violinist and conductor.*

- What's the difference between being silly and being rude?
- Is it rude to tell someone they look old?
- Is it OK to make silly faces at people?

- Have you ever pulled tongues at anyone?
- Who would you like to blow a raspberry at?

> **(GPCH)** I go to my grandchildren. They keep their grandpa informed on what's going on. *Ben Vereen, actor, dancer, and singer.*

Your Call!

Fill in the blanks to make your own conversation starters:

- If you had lots of money would you buy _____?
- If I did this: _____, would you tell me off?
- Have you ever eaten _____?
- If you had a week where you could do anything you wanted, would you _____?
- If you lost your _____ would you be upset?

> **(GPCH)** That's the privilege of being a grandparent—they can indulge the children while parents have to be the bad guy. *Toby Stephens, actor.*

- If someone called you _____ would you find it funny?
- If you were feeling bored, would you go to _____?
- When you were a child did you ever _____?
- If a famous person asked you to _____ would you do it?
- If I gave you a _____ would you use it?

> **(GPCH)** If becoming a grandmother was only a matter of choice, I should advise every one of you straight away to become one. There is no fun for old people like it! *Hannah Whitall Smith, lay speaker and author.*

SECTION 2

For grandparents to ask their grandchildren

School and High School

School

- What do you like best about your school?
- What would you change about your school if you could?
- Tell me about your teacher(s).
- What do you do at recess and lunch time?
- Who's your best friend at school? What fun things do you do together?

> **(GPCH)** Children's talent to endure stems from their ignorance of alternatives. *Maya Angelou, author and poet.*

High School

- Is high school much different from school?
- If you could spend twice the amount of time on one of your subjects and half the amount of time on another, which ones would you choose?
- Which teacher is the coolest?
- Apart from school subjects, what other activities do you do in school?
- What are the other kids like at high school?

(GPCH) Any kid will run any errand for you if you ask at bedtime. *Red Skelton, entertainer and comedian.*

Favorites

- What is your favorite book?
- What is your favorite TV program or movie?
- What is your favorite game?
- What is your favorite animal?
- What is your favorite item of all time?

(GPCH) Children need the freedom and time to play. Play is not a luxury. Play is a necessity. *Kay Redfield Jamison, clinical psychologist and writer.*

- What is your favorite song?
- What is your favorite color?
- Which are your favorite clothes and shoes?
- Do you have a favorite cuddly toy?
- Who is your favorite cartoon character?

(GPCH) At certain historic moments, grandparents took on childrearing responsibilities. In many cultures, they still do. Chinese grandparents who are able to retire at 55 are seen all over Beijing bouncing grandbabies. In the United States, we can't afford to retire at 55. *Erica Jong, author and teacher.*

Home and Interests

Home

- What do you like best about your bedroom?
- If you could have a pet that you kept in your bedroom, real or imagined, what would you have?
- Are there any places at home where you can hide?
- What jobs do you have to do around the house?

- What's the most interesting thing can you see from any of the windows in your house?

> **(GPCH)** I've been accused of being old before my time more than once. It's true that I've always felt an affinity for, and been comfortable around, older people. I attribute this to a childhood spent around my grandparents—and even a great-grandparent or two. I wouldn't trade those experiences for anything. *Jon Meacham, executive editor.*

Interests

- What's your favorite hobby?
- Have you won any awards for your hobbies?
- If you didn't have to go to school, what would you like to do instead?
- What new hobby or interest would you like to try?
- What kind of hobby would you never want to do? Why not?

> **(GPCH)** I was brought up by my grandparents. So people go, "Oh, what was that like? That must have been hard." And you go: "No, it wasn't." It was just completely actually normal because the new norm seems to be whatever you make of it, doesn't it? *James McAvoy, Scottish actor.*

Good Things

- What has been your best day ever?
- What has your mom or dad or teacher said you are good at?
- What's made you laugh the most?
- What do you like best about school vacation?
- If you were given $1000 what would you spend it on?

> **(GPCH)** Grandparents who want to be truly helpful will do well to keep their mouths shut and their opinions to themselves until these are requested. *T. Berry Brazelton, pediatrician and author.*

- What's the best thing about your best friend?
- What would be the perfect day at school?
- What makes you very, very happy?
- What has been your best present?
- What's the kindest thing you've done for someone?

(GPCH) Children are unpredictable. You never know what inconsistency they're going to catch you in next. *Franklin P. Jones, reporter, public relations executive, and humorist.*

Silly Questions

- If you could swap someone in your class at school for an animal, who would you swap and what animal would you get?
- If there was a competition for being the best at burping, how would you do?
- If you had to play a trick on your teacher and make them a silly sandwich, what would you put in it?
- If you could have eyes on the end of your fingers, what would you do?
- If you had some face paints and had to paint your best friend's face, what would you paint on it?

(GPCH) There was never a child so lovely but his mother was glad to get him to sleep. *Ralph Waldo Emerson, essayist, lecturer, and poet.*

- If you had a pet that was a bit of a cat and a bit of a mouse and a bit of a hedgehog, what noise would it make and what would it do?
- If you could dress up as a scary monster, what would you wear and who would you scare?
- What's the worst food in the world? Can you invent a food that is *even worse* than this?

- If you had to hide a HUGE bag of chocolates or candies in your house so that no one knew where they were, where would you hide them?
- If you had to pretend to be a bossy king or queen and give orders to everyone in your family, what would you tell them to do?

> **(GPCH)** Pausing to listen to an airplane in the sky, stooping to watch a ladybug on a plant, sitting on a rock to watch the waves crash over the quayside—children have their own agendas and timescales. As they find out more about their world and their place in it, they work hard not to let adults hurry them. We need to hear their voices. *Cathy Nutbrown, professor and author.*

Growing Up

- What do you want to do when you leave school?
- What would be a fun way to earn your living?
- Is there a particular age you are looking forward to so you can do the things you want to?
- What do you hope your life will be like in five or ten years' time?
- What will be the good parts about being an adult?

> **(GPCH)** Children are great imitators. So give them something great to imitate. *Author Unknown.*

- What will be the difficult parts about being an adult?
- When you are my age, what do you think life will be like?
- Is there anything you would like to change in the world to make it a better place for when you are grown up?
- Which of your friends do you think you'll still be friends with when you are adults?
- Do you have any questions about growing up?

> **(GPCH)** Do not educate your child to be rich, educate them to be happy, so when they grow up they'll know the value of things not the price. *Author Unknown.*

This and That

- What's the best thing about being a child?
- If you could grant someone their wish, who would it be and what have they wished for?
- Where would you most like to go on vacation?
- How much allowance should children get? And what should they spend it on?
- If you could meet someone famous, who would it be? What would you want to do with them or ask them?

(GPCH) Kids in a home with grandparents are healthier. *Dan Buettner, explorer, educator, author, and public speaker.*

- Is there a character from a book, movie, or game you would like to meet?
- If you could star in a film you've seen, which film would it be and what role would you play?
- If you become a grandparent what will you do with your grandkids?
- What's the most annoying thing ever?
- Do you like ghost stories?

(GPCH) Knowing more about family history is the single biggest predictor of a child's emotional well-being. Grandparents can play a special role in this process, too. *Bruce Feiler, writer and television personality.*

Your Family: Grandparents

- What do you think I do during the day when you are at school?
- What makes me laugh a lot?
- What was I good at when I was at school?
- What naughty things do you think I did when I was a kid?
- Do you think I do naughty things now?

> **(GPCH)** To become a grandparent is to enjoy one of the few pleasures in life for which the consequences have already been paid. *Robert Brault, writer.*

- Do you think I'm ticklish?
- Do you think I snore? What would my snores sound like?
- What are the funniest things I do with you?
- If I was going to go to a fancy dress party, what do you think I should wear?
- If I won a million dollars what should I do?

> **(GPCH)** Children are the hands by which we take hold of heaven. *Henry Ward Beecher, reverend and social activist.*

Your Family: Mom

- What's your mom's favorite food?
- What would your mom say if you gave her a spider?
- Have you seen photos of your mom when she was younger? What did she look like?
- What does your mom do if you are feeling unhappy?
- What kind of clothes does your mom buy for herself?

> **(GPCH)** To a small child, the perfect granddad is unafraid of big dogs and fierce storms but absolutely terrified of the word "boo." *Robert Brault, writer.*

- Who is your mom's best friend?
- If you played hide and seek with your mom, where do you think she would hide?
- Is there anything your mom likes you to help her with?
- What makes your mom laugh?
- Which famous person does your mom most look like?

> **(GPCH)** A child needs a grandparent, anybody's grandparent, to grow a little more securely into an unfamiliar world. *Charles and Ann Morse, authors.*

Your Family: Dad

- What's your dad like when he wakes up in the morning?
- What's the coolest thing your dad can do?
- Has your dad got any funny habits?
- Does your dad like to eat any strange foods?
- If your dad was a superhero, which one would he be?

(GPCH) What children need most are the essentials that grandparents provide in abundance. They give unconditional love, kindness, patience, humor, comfort, lessons in life. And, most importantly, cookies. *Rudolph Giuliani, American lawyer, businessman, and former politician.*

- How does your dad laugh? Can you make the same laughing sound?
- What do you think your dad was like when he was a little boy?
- Tell me about something brave your dad has done.
- What games does your dad like to play with you?
- What would be a real good present to buy for your dad?

(GPCH) A grandmother is a babysitter who watches the kids instead of the television. *Author Unknown.*

Fun Questions

- If you could be a new superhero with any superpower at all, who would you be and what superpower would you have?
- What's the funniest thing you've ever done?
- What's the grossest thing you've ever seen?
- If you could choose to have as many brothers and sisters as you liked and could choose how old they were, what would you choose?
- If you could spend the day doing whatever you liked and your mom or dad had to agree to it, what would you do?

> **(GPCH)** No cowboy was ever faster on the draw than a grandparent pulling a baby picture out of a wallet. *Author Unknown.*

- What does the Tooth Fairy do with all the teeth?
- If your teddy or your favorite toy came to life, what would you do together?
- If you had a magic carpet where would you go?
- If you had to make a den out of pillows cushions and sheets, and then take some food and some games in there, what would you take?
- If someone asked you to do something goofy so they could take a photo of you, what would you do?

> **(GPCH)** A house needs a grandma in it. *Louisa May Alcott, American novelist.*

Tell a Story

Make up a story for younger children using the story starters. As well as being another way to strengthen bonds, a story can also act as a conversation starter.

- Once upon a time, there was a witch who had hair made of string ...
- "Surprise!" said the boy's parents when he woke up one morning ...
- Grandma had a secret place where she hid all the interesting types of food that children like ...
- The little boy was in his bedroom when he heard the jingling noise of Santa's sleigh ...
- One day Bella the puppy did something very naughty ...

> **(GPCH)** Listen earnestly to anything your children want to tell you, no matter what. If you don't listen eagerly to the little stuff when they are little they won't tell you the big stuff when they are big, because to them all of it has always been big stuff. *Catherine M. Wallace, author, poet, and essayist.*

- "I don't like cabbage!" said Poppy, folding her arms and looking very grumpy …
- Once upon a time there was a boy who liked to make rude noises …
- Granddad kept lots of interesting things in his shed. One day he held something up and said, "This is a magic hammer"…
- "I can't find my teddy!" cried the little girl …
- One day Fluffy the bunny decided to have an adventure …

> **(GPCH)** When a child is born, so are grandmothers. *Judith Levy, attorney.*

Joint Stories (1)

You and your grandchild can make up a story together. Let them start, and then you can take turns.

- Once upon a time there was a little boy who wanted to have the biggest birthday cake in the world.
- One day a magic fairy waved her wand and said to the little girl, "I grant you one wish. You can wish for anything you want. What would you like?"
- One day Bobby found a big golden box at the end of his bed.
- Once upon a time there was a girl called Anne whose hair grew and grew and GREW until it reached all the way down to the ground.

> **(GPCH)** Becoming a grandmother is wonderful. One moment you're just a mother. The next you are all-wise and prehistoric. *Pam Brown, poet.*

- Once upon a time a huge, enormous elephant tried to sit on a swing.
- One night time, when it was very, very dark, an alien spaceship landed on our lawn.
- One day I heard a very strange noise coming from the house next door.

- Once upon a time there was a very cheeky boy who used to say the word "snigglebum."
- Once upon a time there was a big, big giant who liked to eat jelly beans.
- One day all the children in the class went on a treasure hunt.

(GPCH) There's no place like home except Grandma's. *Author Unknown.*

Joint Stories (2)

You and your grandchild can choose two of these words or phrases each and make up a joint story:

- TEDDY – ADVENTURE – NIGHT TIME – FOREST
- WICKED WITCH – MOUNTAIN TOP – FROGS – EVIL LAUGH
- PARTY – CLOWN – TRUMPET – BICYCLE
- DESERT – VERY THIRSTY – CAMEL – MAGIC CARPET
- SIX ALIENS – BROKEN SPACESHIP – TRACTOR – COWS

(GPCH) Being grandparents sufficiently removes us from the responsibilities so that we can be friends. *Allan Frome, author.*

- HAIRY MONSTER – SINGING – LAMP POST – POLICEMAN
- AIRPLANE – WIZARD – STRANGE WEATHER – DISAPPEAR
- HORSE RIDING – STREAM – ELF – BONFIRE
- DRAGON – BRAVE WARRIOR – FLYING – OCEAN
- OLD, OLD MAN – HEDGEHOG – PANCAKES – GENIE

(GPCH) An aware parent loves all children he or she interacts with—for you are a caretaker for those moments in time. *Doc Childre, founder of HeartMath.*

Thinking

Either let your grandchild answer these on their own or work on them together, and find out how your grandchild thinks, plans, and solves problems:

- Let's plan the best day out ever. What shall we do?
- If you could have anything in your bedroom that you wanted, what would you have?
- Imagine someone gave you three puppies and three kittens and asked you to choose names for them. What names would you choose?
- Imagine we were going to go for a day out at the beach, what would we need to take with us?
- Imagine we were going to plan a special surprise for your mom or dad's birthday, what could we organize?

(GPCH) When grandparents enter the door, discipline flies out the window. *Ogden Nash, American poet.*

- If we had three apples and there were four children, and all the children wanted an apple, what would we do?
- If your teacher asked all the children in your class to draw a red boat, but one of the children drew a green airplane instead, what should the teacher do?
- Imagine you are a detective and have found a bag. You have to look at the items inside and work out who it belongs to. In the bag you find: a magazine about fishing; a comb; a diaper and some wipes; the crust off a sandwich; a plastic toy; two train tickets; a water bottle; and some keys. Who could the bag belong to?
- If someone gave you some Play-Doh, some Popsicle sticks, and a hundred colored beads and asked you to make something interesting, what would you make?
- Imagine someone gave you a scrapbook, scissors and glue, and lots of different types of comics. Then they asked you to cut out some pictures and make up an interesting book; what kind of book would you make?

> **(GPCH)** Children are the living messages we send to a time we will not see. *John W. Whitehead, founder, Rutherford Institute.*

Creative Questions

These are fun conversation starters that let you and your grandchild work on creative thinking together. Some children are great creative thinkers, able to look at things from different angles, and come up with new ideas or ways of doing things. It's also a good chance for you to get the creative juices flowing and try new and different ways of thinking.

Introduce this section by telling your grandchild that you are both going to have fun working out answers to unusual questions. If they can't or don't want to tackle these topics, that's OK, just move onto something else.

- If trees could walk, where would they walk to?
- If the moon could speak, what would it say?
- What kinds of animals might like to eat clouds?
- What do elephants dream about?
- What do your toys do when you are asleep?

> **(GPCH)** Everybody knows how to raise children, except the people who have them. *P. J. O'Rourke, political satirist, journalist, writer, and author.*

- What would the sun do if it got cold?
- What would happen if our legs were made out of rubber and we could roll them up?
- If a friendly ghost invited you to its birthday, what would happen at the party?
- What would happen if your bed was made out of chocolate?
- What would happen if rain was made of sugar?

> **(GPCH)** It's one of nature's ways that we often feel closer to distant generations than to the generation immediately preceding us. *Igor Stravinsky, composer, pianist, and conductor.*

Your Future

For teenagers and older grandchildren:

- Tell me about your career plans.
- What qualifications do you think you'll wind up with?
- Can you imagine being in a long-term relationship or marriage?
- Would you like to have children in the future?
- Can you imagine yourself being a grandparent in the future?

> **(GPCH)** Grandmas bring flowers when your pet dies...and sit and cry with you. *Author Unknown.*

- When would you like to leave home?
- What kind of house do you imagine yourself living in when you are older?
- If you could be famous for achieving something extraordinary, what would you like to be famous for?
- Which of your skills and interests will be the most useful for your future?
- Is there anything I can do to help you move forward in life?

> **(GPCH)** Let us sacrifice our today so that our children can have a better tomorrow. *Abdul Kalam, scientist and administrator.*

Teenagers

For teenagers and older grandchildren:

- What are the issues facing teenagers today?
- Do teenagers get bad publicity in the media, unfairly?
- Is it hard for people to be parents of teenagers these days?
- What are your views on the politics of your country?
- How important is education and qualifications for people's future?

(GPCH) Being pretty on the inside means you don't hit your brother and you eat all your peas—that's what my grandma taught me. *Lord Chesterfield, British Statesman.*

- If a teenager has few qualifications and no desire to gain any, what else can they do to create a good future for themselves?
- How easy is it for teenagers entering the workforce to find a job?
- What qualities make someone a really great employee?
- How big is the drug problem for teenagers these days?
- Why are more and more adolescents becoming obese?

(GPCH) You do not really understand something unless you can explain it to your grandmother. *Proverb.*

... In the World

- What is the best food in the world?
- If I could take you to the biggest toy shop in the world, what would you buy?
- Would you like to be the tallest person in the world?
- What would the best playground in the world be like?
- If you were the richest person in the world, what would you do with your money?

(GPCH) It's amazing how grandparents seem so young once you become one. *Author Unknown.*

- What would the biggest sandwich in the world have in it?
- What would be the best job in the world?
- What would be the worst job in the world?
- If you had the biggest party in the world, who would you invite and what would happen at the party?
- What is the most amazing creature in the world?

(**GPCH**) Grandparents are there to help the child get into mischief they haven't thought of yet. *Gene Perret, comedy writer.*

Activities

Consider doing an activity with your grandchild and letting the conversation flow from that. You may simply have a general conversation while you are doing an activity, or you could choose an activity and a specific topic and center the conversation around that. In this way the focus is on the activity, with conversation arising naturally from it, rather than the focus being on "having a conversation." This strategy will suit some children (and adults!) better. It can work well for those who are shy or are not natural conversationalists.

The following are examples of ways to use an activity to incorporate a topic, along with sample conversation starters and questions. Bring in your own questions relevant to the child or the situation and let the conversation flow from there.

There are many other activities and topics this technique can be used with.

- Activity: Drawing or painting.

Topic: School
"Let's do some drawing or painting. How about I draw the school and you can draw your teacher? What does your teacher look like? What color hair has she got? What type of clothes does she wear? Does she smile much?

Now let's draw some children in your class. Who do you sit next to? What does he/she look like? What's he/she good at? Is he/she friendly? Does he/she have a loud voice?"

And so on…

- Activity: Play-Doh.

Topic: Pets
"OK, you roll the Play-Doh and get it nice and soft and then we can make a model of _____ [insert name of child's pet]. What colors shall we use?

Is _____ big or small? What kind of tail does he/she have?

*Where does _____ sleep? What noise does he/she make when
he's/she's happy?*
Does _____ do anything naughty?"
And so on…

- Activity: I Spy.

Topic: Toys
Play this wherever your grandchild keeps their toys. Ask the children
to do an "I Spy" for some of their toys. When it's your turn, you
can do an "I Spy" for something in the room other than toys—for
example lamp, cushion, or window—so that they don't get confused.
When it's their turn, ask them to do an "I Spy" for:

Their favorite toy
Their favorite game
Their favorite cuddly toy
A toy that has yellow in it
A toy that was a present from a friend
A toy from Santa
And so on…

- Activity: Quiz.

Topic: Friends and family
Have a list of characteristics and write each one on a card or piece
of paper. Put them in a bag, pull out one at a time, and ask each other
which friend or family member fits the description. Then explain why,
or say something about it.
The cards can say, for example:
Who do you know who:

- Loves animals
- Likes to eat vegetables
- Doesn't like sports
- Is very tall
- Watches a lot of TV
- Has nice clothes
- Has many brothers and sisters
- Is very helpful
- Laughs a lot

- Talks in a loud voice
- Has been on an exciting vacation
- Has a cool hairstyle

And so on…

- Activity: Memory game.

Topic: Favorite characters
This is a chance for your grandchild to share with you their favorite characters from TV, books, games, or movies.

Ask your grandchild to start, for example: *"I went to the mall and I saw Pikachu."*

Then you go next, *"I went to the mall and I saw Pikachu and Bugs Bunny."*

They carry on, *"I went to the mall and I saw Pikachu, Bugs Bunny and Spiderman."*

And so on…

You may like to get up to speed with some characters for when it's your turn! For example: Dora the Explorer, Elmo, Big Bird, Pikachu, Ash, The Simpsons, SpongeBob SquarePants, Harry Potter, The Smurfs, Batman, Cinderella, Arthur, Spiderman, Mickey Mouse, Bugs Bunny, The Cat in the Hat, The Grinch, My Little Pony, Yogi Bear, Winnie the Pooh, Scooby-Doo, Garfield, Buzz Lightyear, Woody, The Incredibles, Max and Ruby, Franklin, The Very Hungry Caterpillar, Peppa Pig, Wally, The Gruffalo. There are many more!

> **(GPCH)** I have a warm feeling after playing with my grandchildren. It's the liniment working. *Author Unknown.*

- Activity: Crouch and stretch.

Topic: Young to old
The aim is to find out what your grandchild remembers about being young, through to the age they are now, and then what they want to do when they are older.

Start off crouching as low as you can. The first person says, *"When I was a baby …"* and then ideally relates an incident, for example, *"When I was a baby, my mom said I used to laugh when my brother made funny faces."* If they can't relate an incident, say something general, such as, *"When I was a baby I used to sleep in a crib."*

The next person does the same.

Then crouch a bit higher (have a chair handy in case you need to hold on!) and say something about being a bit older: *"When I was at kindergarten / school I ..."*

Continue until you are standing upright, and are talking about life at present.

Finish off by standing on your toes, reaching as high as you can and saying, *"When I'm older I'm going to ..."*

- Activity: Ball toss.

Topic: Food and drink

Either sit or stand and throw a ball to each other, or throw a ball into a container such as a waste bin. Ideally have several balls. Each time someone throws a ball, they have to choose a type of food and say if they like it or not. For example, *"I like apple pie"* or *"I like cold milk"* or *"I don't like peas."*

You don't need to do this quickly; you can play it slowly so that the child has time to think.

- Activity: Dance.

Topic: Million dollars

Play some music for a short while, as you both dance. When the music ends, stop dancing and one of you has to say, *"If I had a million dollars I would ..."*

Then start the music and dancing again and the next person has to say *"If I had a million dollars I would ..."* when the music ends.

See what you find out about each other!

- Activity: Clap and speak.

Topic: Being cheeky

The first person claps three times as quietly as they can, and says in their quietest whisper, *"One day I did a cheeky thing, I ..."* and shares a mildly cheeky thing they've done, for example didn't make their bed or didn't finish their dinner. The next person does the same.

When it's the first person's turn again, this time they clap and whisper slightly louder, and again share a cheeky thing they have done.

Carry on until you are both clapping and speaking as loudly as you can!

- Activity: Objects.

Topic: Special meanings

Each of you chooses a few objects that are special to you, for example a photo, an award, a book, a gift, an item of clothing.

Take turns showing the other person the object and explaining the special meaning it has for you.

(GPCH) Grandmother-grandchild relationships are simple. Grandmas are short on criticism and long on love. *Author Unknown.*

Let's Pretend

- Let's pretend you are the grandparent and I'm the grandchild. What should I do today?
- Let's pretend you are the grandparent and I'm the grandchild and I didn't eat my food or tidy my room. What would you say?
- Let's pretend we are sailors on a boat and we have just seen a pirate boat with scary pirates on it.
- Let's pretend we have to make up a show to perform for your mom and dad. What shall we do?
- Let's pretend that you are one of the Three Little Pigs and I'm the Big Bad Wolf.

(GPCH) "You're more trouble than the children are" is the greatest compliment a grandparent can receive. *Gene Perret, comedy writer.*

- Let's pretend that I've gone into a haunted house and you are the ghost.
- Let's pretend that you have magic powers and have put a spell on me.
- Let's pretend that I have magic powers and have put a spell on you.

- Let's pretend that we are brave knights going through the forest to save a princess in a tower.
- Let's pretend that we are explorers going through the jungle.

> **(GPCH)** A grandmother pretends she doesn't know who you are on Halloween. *Erma Bombeck, humorist and author.*

Discussion Topics

Read out the following scenarios, have a chat about them, and ask what your grandchild might do or what their thoughts are:

- You buy something from a shop and the assistant gives you too much change.
- You arrive at your house, no one is home, and you have forgotten your key.
- You are walking along the street; a man you don't know stops his car and offers you a gift.
- You discover that someone has stolen something out of your bag while you are at school.
- One of your friends at school hasn't done their homework and asks if they can copy yours.

> **(GPCH)** I like to do nice things for my grandchildren—like buy them those toys I've always wanted to play with. *Gene Perret, comedy writer.*

- You receive a Valentine's card and don't know who it's from.
- The local TV station is making a program on schools in the area. The TV crew comes into your classroom and asks what you think about school.
- One of your friends has lost their mobile phone and asks if they can borrow yours for the weekend.
- You get to school and realize you are wearing shoes that don't match.

- A friend comes to see you, bringing their kid brother with them. The brother goes into your bedroom and messes it up.

> **(GPCH)** A mother becomes a true grandmother the day she stops noticing the terrible things her children do because she is so enchanted with the wonderful things her grandchildren do. *Lois Wyse, advertising executive, author, and columnist.*

What Would You Do If?

- What would you do if you found out you were a prince or a princess?
- What would you do if you were asked to be in a show and play the part of a clown?
- What would you do if you were offered money to be in a TV advert if you shaved your hair and eyebrows off?
- What would you do if you were asked to look after your neighbors' very large pet snake for a week while they went away?
- What would you do if you found a frog in your bed?

> **(GPCH)** I have never once regretted missing a business opportunity so that I could be with my children and grandchildren. *Mitt Romney, American businessman and politician.*

- What would you do if you couldn't watch TV for a year?
- What would you do if you started a new school and got the nickname "Superhero"?
- What would you do if a big fluffy cat came to your house every day and looked like it wanted to live with you?
- What would you do if you did your homework and then the neighbor's dog ate it?
- What would you do if you found a goldfish in the toilet?

> **(GPCH)** Elephants and grandchildren never forget. *Andy Rooney, American radio and television writer.*

Fun!

- Imagine we were invisible and could travel for free on any bus, train, or plane and go into any place for free because no one could see us. What would you like to do?
- Imagine we were very important people and could live in a big palace for a weekend. We would have servants who could bring us anything we wanted and we could do anything we liked. What would we do?
- Can you think of a funny practical joke you would like to play on someone?
- If we could go camping together and take lots of food and games to play, what would you take?
- Would it be fun to dress up as a ghost, go to the mall, and shout "Boo!" at people?

> **(GPCH)** If my grandchildren were to look at me and say, "You were aware species were disappearing and you did nothing, you said nothing," that I think is culpable. I don't know how much more they expect me to be doing, I'd better ask them. *David Attenborough, English broadcaster and naturalist.*

- If you could get fancy dress outfits for all the teachers at your school, which outfits would you choose?
- What would happen if a clown came into your classroom with a hundred custard pies?
- What would be the most fun job in the world?
- If you had a big photo of someone's face and could draw on it to make it look funny, what would you draw?
- What could be the most fun kind of party you could have for your next birthday?

> **(GPCH)** Never have children, only grandchildren. *Gore Vidal, writer and public intellectual.*

This and That

- If you could only eat one type of food for two whole days at breakfast, lunch, and dinner, what would you eat?
- If you were going on a long trip, would you rather travel in a car, a train, a plane, a helicopter, a boat, or a hot air balloon?
- Which of these jobs sounds the most interesting and why: a zookeeper, a pilot, a teacher, a singer, or a doctor?
- What do you like to have for breakfast?
- How would you feel if your mom or dad decided to become a teacher and teach your class?

(GPCH) Your sons weren't made to like you. That's what grandchildren are for. *Jane Smiley, American novelist.*

- What would you do if you were lying in bed and saw a big spider on the ceiling above your head?
- If you had to go from one side of the room to the other, but instead of walking you had to do it in other ways, how many ways can you think of?
- Who do you know who talks too much?
- If you had a time machine and could go back to the time of the dinosaurs, would you go?
- If you had a cloak that made you invisible for a day, what would you do?

(GPCH) Each day of our lives we make deposits in the memory banks of our children. *Charles R. Swindoll, pastor, author, and educator.*

Magic Wand

- If you had a magic wand and could do cool spells, what spell would you do?
- If you had a magic wand, what things would you change about your house?

- If you had a magic wand, which character from a book, TV, or movie would you like to come to your house?
- If you had a magic wand and could change your clothes and shoes right now, what would they look like?
- If you had a magic wand and could look like whoever or whatever you wanted, what would you look like?

> **(GPCH)** Few things are more delightful than grandchildren fighting over your lap. *Doug Larson, columnist and editor.*

- If you had a magic wand and could invent a new type of food that every child would want to eat, what food would it be?
- If you had a magic wand, what new toys or games would you have?
- If you had a magic wand and could give someone three wishes, who would you give them to?
- If you had a magic wand, where would you like to be right now?
- If you had a magic wand, how would you change your school to make it the most fun school in the world?

> **(GPCH)** Grandchildren are God's way of compensating us for growing old. *Mary H. Waldrip, English nurse.*

Scenarios (1) for younger children

Read out the scenario, and help your grandchild answer the question about it:

- It's bedtime for a young girl. Her mom takes her to the bedroom, but instead of getting into bed the girl crawls under the bed and won't come out. Why did the girl do this?
- A girl goes to her friend's house and takes her teddy bear. Her friend's brother throws her teddy out of the window. What should the girl do?

- A granddad takes his grandson to the park. They stop to have lunch. The boy won't eat his sandwich and wants to have an ice cream instead. Is that OK?
- A mom and dad are taking their children to the movies as a treat. Just before they leave the house one of the children gets into a bad mood and breaks an ornament. Should the mom and dad stop all the children from going to the movie?
- A girl opens the fridge door and some eggs fall out and smash onto the floor. Her dad gets annoyed and tells her off. Why does her dad get angry?

> **(GPCH)** What a bargain grandchildren are! I give them my loose change, and they give me a million dollars' worth of pleasure. *Gene Perret, comedy writer.*

- Two children are playing at school. One of them wears glasses. The other child says, "I don't like your glasses." Is it OK to say this?
- A boy pretends to be ill so that he doesn't have to go to school. Instead he stays home and watches TV. Later, his mom realizes he's pretending. The next week the boy really is ill but his mom doesn't know if she can believe him. Will she make him go to school?
- One of the boys at school is being silly. A girl shouts at him, saying, "All boys are stupid." Is it OK to say this?
- A girl loses one of her special toys and starts to cry. Her brother says, "Don't be dumb, it's just an old toy." Why does he say that?
- Two boys are playing in the street with a ball. A girl comes along, takes their ball, and throws it into the bushes. What should the boys do?

> **(GPCH)** It is easier to build strong children than to repair broken men. *Frederick Douglass, African-American social reformer, orator, writer, and statesman.*

Scenarios (2) for teenagers

Read out the scenario, and ask your grandchild what they think about it or what should happen:

- A teenage girl wears a lot of make-up and spends large amounts of time doing her hair. She says to a girl who doesn't do this, "You should make more of your appearance, you look very plain."
- A teenage boy at high school has all the latest technology games and gadgets. He belittles one of his classmates—in front of other students—whose family can't afford to do this.
- One of your friends is regularly being cyberbullied by a classmate but is too afraid to tell anyone apart from you.
- A teenager likes to spend a lot of time online hanging out with mates or playing games. His parents try to stop him from using the computer and nag him all the time, saying things like, "Stop wasting your life."
- You wonder if one of your classmates is being physically abused because you've seen the bruises on their body in the changing rooms.

> **(GPCH)** You better arm yourselves to answer your children's and grandchildren's questions... no matter what the question is... without being judgmental. *Josh McDowell, Christian apologist, evangelist, and writer.*

- A sixteen year old wants to go to a party but his parents won't let him because they think there will be alcohol there.
- An 18-year-old girl is about to leave high school but doesn't know what job or career to follow. She hasn't done well in her studies.
- One of your friends is very slim but thinks she is fat and so hardly eats any lunch.
- Your 17-year-old friend wants to ask a girl out on a date but doesn't think he stands a chance.
- You and your friends are 18 and want to go on vacation together but none of you has much money.

> **(GPCH)** You have to love your children unselfishly. That is hard. But it is the only way. *Barbara Bush, former U.S. first lady.*

Your Call!

Fill in the blanks to make your own conversation starters:

- If you found a _____ under your bed, what would you do?
- Would you like to go to _____?
- If I gave you _____ to eat, what would you do?
- If I gave you a _____, what would you do with it?
- If (*insert name of famous person*) _____ asked you out on a date, what would you say?

> **(GPCH)** Children are likely to live up to what you believe of them. *Lady Bird Johnson, former U.S. first lady.*

- If I offered to take you and a friend to _____ which friend would you bring?
- How many _____ are there in your bedroom?
- What do you think about _____?
- What's the most _____ gift you've received?
- If you had a lot of money would you spend it on _____?

> **(GPCH)** A child seldom needs a good talking to as a good listening to. *Robert Brault, writer.*

SECTION 3

For grandparents to ask their adult children

Being a Parent

- When you were growing up, did you ever think about having children?
- Did you learn anything about how to be a good parent when you were at school?
- What did you think parenting would be like before you had children? And is it how you imagined?
- What has been the most rewarding part of being a parent?
- What has been the most challenging part of being a parent?

> **(GPCH)** Children begin by loving their parents; as they grow older they judge them; sometimes they forgive them. *Oscar Wilde, Irish writer and poet.*

- Have you discovered anything about yourself since becoming a parent?
- Have you discovered anything about your husband, wife or partner since they became a parent?
- What has been the most touching or significant incident or aspect since you became a parent?
- If you could start out again as a parent, is there anything you would change?
- What are your dreams and aspirations for your children?

(**GPCH**) If there were no schools to take the children away from home part of the time, the insane asylums would be filled with mothers. *Edgar W. Howe, novelist and editor.*

Parenting, Grandparenting, and Family

- What is the ideal grandparent like?
- Is there anything I could do to be a better grandparent?
- Is there anything we could do together for the grandchildren?
- Is there anything you would like me to do for you or the grandchildren?
- Are you happy for us to give treats to the children?

(**GPCH**) Cleaning your house while your kids are still growing up is like shoveling the walk before it stops snowing. *Phyllis Diller, comedienne, actress, and voice artist.*

- How big a part should a child's aunts, uncles and cousins play in their life?
- Is there anyone in the family you would like your children to spend more time with?
- Is there anyone in the family you would like your children to spend less time with?
- What do the children feel about family gatherings?
- Some cultures share the parenting role among family members. Does that appeal to you?

(**GPCH**) Anyone who thinks the art of conversation is dead ought to tell a child to go to bed. *Robert Gallagher, author.*

SECTION 4

For grandparent couples to ask each other

Early Days

- When did you first notice me? And what did you think?
- What was our most memorable date?
- What was my most endearing quality?
- Can you remember any of the clothes you liked me to wear?
- What made you decide that you wanted to marry or be with me?

(CP) I love being married. It's so great to find that one special person you want to annoy for the rest of your life. *Rita Rudner, comedienne, writer, and actress.*

- What did you think of my family when you met them?
- How would you describe the proposal?
- What were your thoughts about having children in the early days?
- Did you ever think ahead to us being older or being grandparents?
- Have we both changed much since the early days?

(CP) Newlyweds become oldyweds, and oldyweds are the reasons that families work. *Author Unknown.*

About You and Me (1)

What do you know about each other's early years?

- What was my career ambition when I was younger?
- What was I scared of when I was a child?
- What was family life like for me when I was growing up?
- Which schools did I go to?
- What school subject was I best at?

(CP) Ideally, couples need three lives; one for him, one for her, and one for them together. *Jacqueline Bisset, English actress.*

- What did I get into trouble for?
- Did I win any awards?
- Did I have any pets?
- Did I get pocket money?
- Did I have a heartthrob?

(CP) This would be a much better world if more married couples were as deeply in love as they are in debt. *Earl Wilson, journalist, columnist, and author.*

About You and Me (2)

Do you know each other as well as you think?

- What color are my eyes?
- What would I like as a treat for my birthday?
- What's my favorite color?
- What do I keep in my purse or wallet?
- What's my biggest fear?

(CP) Marriage is a wonderful invention: then again, so is a bicycle repair kit. *Billy Connolly, Scottish comedian, musician, presenter, and actor.*

- Which part of my body bothers me the most?
- What time of day do I like best?

- What's my favorite season?
- Which part of the newspaper do I read first?
- What is my shoe size?

(CP) Research shows that couples who have a lot of similarities, including intellectual compatibility, end up staying together. *Helen Fisher, anthropologist and human behavior researcher.*

About You and Me (3)

How much do you know about your partner?
What choice would I make in these circumstances?

- Would I prefer a night in at home with a movie, or an evening out at a show?
- If I had $1000 would I prefer to go shopping or have a vacation?
- If I entered a competition and won a car, what would I do with it?
- If I had to spend a night in a haunted house or give a talk in front of a thousand people, which would I choose?
- If I could have an evening out with a celebrity, who would I choose?

(CP) Before marriage, many couples are very much like people rushing to catch an airplane; once aboard, they turn into passengers. They just sit there. *Paul Getty, industrialist.*

- If the house was on fire and I could save two items, what would I save?
- If I had to have a profile photo taken, showing my right side or my left side, which would I choose?
- What order of priority would I put these vacation destinations in: The Far East, Africa, Europe?
- If I could become someone else for a day, which of these would I choose to be: a politician, an aid worker, a fire fighter, or a movie star?
- If I could have my life over and choose a different career or occupation, what would I choose?

> **(CP)** That married couples can live together day after day is a miracle that the Vatican has overlooked. *Bill Cosby, comedian, actor, and author.*

Family

- What were your grandparents like?
- What's your favorite memory of your mother?
- What's your favorite memory of your father?
- Do you think your parents had a good parenting style?
- Did you spend much time with aunts, uncles, and other family members?

> **(CP)** I love you. You annoy me more than I ever thought possible, but… I want to spend every irritating minute with you. *From the television series* Scrubs.

- Were you nervous about having children?
- Are there any family members you are worried about?
- Who should be the linchpin person for the extended family?
- Do we have enough family gatherings?
- What's the one thing you would like to happen for the family in the coming year?

> **(CP)** I think it's healthy for couples to be away from each other for short periods. *Liv Tyler, actress and model.*

Grandparenting (1)

- What did you expect grandparenting would be like before you became a grandparent?
- What's the best thing about being a grandparent?
- How do you feel you are doing as a grandparent?
- Has anything about being a grandparent disappointed you?
- Do you worry about the grandchildren?

(CP) If you live to be 100, I hope I live to be 100 minus one day, so I never have to live without you. *Ernest H. Shepard, English artist and book illustrator.*

- What do you think of the names our grandchildren have?
- Are the grandchildren being disciplined enough?
- If you could go back in time and change one thing you've done as a grandparent, what would it be?
- Do you feel you know enough about the things our grandchildren are interested in?
- Now that you are a grandparent, is there anything you wish you'd done differently as a parent?

(CP) A long marriage is two people trying to dance a duet and two solos at the same time. *Anne Taylor Fleming, journalist and novelist.*

Grandparenting (2)

- Do you feel sorry for people who aren't grandparents?
- Do you know anyone who has difficult grandchildren that you feel sorry for?
- Do you wish you had been older or younger when you became a grandparent, or do you think it happened at the right age for you?
- What do you think our children will be like as grandparents?
- Would you like to be a substitute grandparent for local children whose grandparents don't live close by or who don't have grandparents?

(CP) Lasting love has to be built on mutual regard and respect. It is about seeing the other person. I am very interested in relationships and, when I watch couples, sometimes I can sense a blindness has set in. They have stopped seeing each other. It is not easy to see another person. *Chimamanda Ngozi Adichie, Nigerian writer.*

- Do you worry about the amount of inoculations that children receive these days?
- Do our grandchildren get too many gifts at Christmas?
- What could we do when we run out of ideas for things to do with the grandchildren?
- What was your favorite activity when you were a child that you did with your grandparents or parents?
- What do you think of the concept of Grandparents' Day?

(CP) The concept of two people living together for 25 years without a serious dispute suggests a lack of spirit only to be admired in sheep. *A.P. Herbert, English humorist, novelist, and playwright.*

Our Children

- Did we prepare our children enough for parenthood?
- How do you feel about being a mother-in-law / father-in-law?
- Would you say you had a good relationship with your daughter-in-law / son-in-law?
- Do you think the children are doing a good job of parenting?
- How would you describe our children's parenting style?

(CP) You don't develop courage by being happy in your relationships every day. You develop it by surviving difficult times and challenging adversity. *Epicurus, ancient Greek philosopher.*

- Do the children treat us as competent grandparents?
- Do the children give us enough access to the grandchildren?
- Do we treat each of our children differently?
- Has our relationship with our children changed since they became parents?
- Do you fancy doing something to give our son/daughter a break or help with the grandchildren. What could we do?

(CP) In my view, relationship movies never get old because humanity will never not be confounded by their relationships. *Zoe Lister-Jones, actress, singer, playwright, and screenwriter.*

Our Grandchildren

- What has been the best experience you've had with the grandchildren?
- If we were to plan a surprise for the grandchildren, what could we do?
- What are you good at doing with, or for, the grandchildren?
- What am I good at doing with, or for, the grandchildren?
- What would be a perfect gift or experience we could buy or provide for each grandchild?

(CP) All couples have been told to schedule regular one-on-one time. "Date night" is the default answer to most problems in modern marriages. And research backs this up. *Bruce Feiler, writer and television personality.*

- Is there a project we could do with the grandchildren, together or separately?
- If there was one thing we could do for our grandchildren that would be of benefit to them in the future, what would it be?
- Let's do something silly with the grandchildren! What shall we do?
- Can we do something to mark how special our grandchildren are? Perhaps write a poem, do a painting for them, have a special section in the garden for them to plant something …?
- Is there something different we can do for the grandchildren's next birthdays?

(CP) Men should keep their eyes wide open before marriage, and half-shut afterwards. *Madeleine de Scudéry, French writer.*

The Future

- What are you most looking forward to in the near future?
- What will we be doing in five years' time?
- What exciting things can we plan for the next few years?
- Are there things you would like to do with the grandchildren when they are older?
- Are there issues to sort out regarding our financial future?

(CP) Honesty, trust, communication, respect, and understanding. Mix it all together and you have a relationship that works. *Author Unknown.*

- Do we need to do anything to ensure our home and garden is well-maintained?
- Do we need to have a plan regarding moving into a different kind of house or accommodation as we get older?
- Do we need to write or amend our wills?
- Do we need to have strategies or contingency plans regarding our health as we go forward?
- Are we as prepared as we can be for when one of us is no longer here?

(CP) Whenever you're in conflict with someone, there is one factor that can make the difference between damaging your relationship and deepening it. That factor is attitude. *William James, philosopher and psychologist.*

Would You Like...?

Find out a bit more about your partner!

- Would you like to have more grandchildren?
- Would you like to have great grandchildren?
- Would you like to spend more time with the grandchildren?
- Would you like to have more hobbies or interests?
- Would you like to learn a new skill?

> **(CP)** Every good relationship, especially marriage, is based on respect. If it's not based on respect, nothing that appears to be good will last very long. *Amy Grant, musician, author, and actress.*

- Would you like to change your appearance at all?
- Would you like to move house or live somewhere else?
- Would you like to do more education?
- Would you like us to spend more time together?
- Would you like to be young again?

> **(CP)** Well, it seems to me that the best relationships—the ones that last—are frequently the ones that are rooted in friendship. *Gillian Anderson, author.*

Music

- What music reminds you of when we first met or our early days?
- Is there a song that you associate with a significant event?
- What are your top three favorite songs?
- If you could go back in time and see a singer from the past at one of their performances, who would you like to see?
- What type of music did your parents listen to?

> **(CP)** The real act of marriage takes place in the heart, not in the ballroom or church or synagogue. It's a choice you make—not just on your wedding day, but over and over again—and that choice is reflected in the way you treat your husband or wife. *Barbara de Angelis, relationship consultant, lecturer, and author.*

- Which children's song do you like the best?
- Are there any children's songs that drive you mad?
- Do you think the singers today are good role models for our grandchildren?
- Are musical toys for children a good thing?
- Is there a type of music that helps children learn?

(CP) Never feel remorse for what you have thought about your wife; she has thought much worse things about you. *Jean Rostand, biologist and philosopher.*

Who Is...?

Think through all of the members of our family, including those who are no longer with us, and answer the following:

- Who is the most creative or artistic member?
- Who is the most adventurous member?
- Who is the most financially savvy member?
- Who is the most happy-go-lucky member?
- Who is the family member that makes you laugh the most?

(CP) If you want to read about love and marriage, you've got to buy two separate books. *Alan King, actor and comedian.*

- If you were trapped in an elevator with a family member, who is the person best able to cope?
- If you needed advice about how to relate to young children, who is the best person to talk to?
- If you wanted to improve or maintain your health into old age, who is the best person to help you?
- If you wanted an enjoyable day out, who is the best person to go with?
- If you wanted someone to write your memoirs for you, who is the best person to do that?

(CP) A beautiful thing happens when we start paying attention to each other. It is by participating more in your relationship that you breathe life into it. *Author Unknown.*

Parenting and Grandparenting

What differences, if any, are there between being a parent and a grandparent, or being a parent now and a parent in our day?

- Do you worry less about our grandchildren than you would if they were our children?
- Do you feel as protective towards our grandchildren as you did towards our children?
- Do you feel you can discipline the grandchildren as much as you would if they were your children?
- Are you as strict as a grandparent as you were as a parent?
- Do you think the same way about bedtime routines for the grandchildren as you did for the children?

(CP) When a man opens the car door for his wife, it's either a new car or a new wife. *Prince Philip, husband of Queen Elizabeth II.*

- Do you give the grandchildren more treats than you did the children?
- What effect does technology have on parenting nowadays that didn't happen when we were first parents?
- What problems do parents these days have to deal with that we didn't?
- Did our children miss out on anything that our grandchildren take for granted?
- Do parents these days need more money to buy what children now regard as essential?

(CP) A great marriage is not when the "perfect couple" comes together. It is when an imperfect couple learns to enjoy their differences. *Dave Meurer, humor writer.*

SECTION 5

For grandparents in general conversation

Being a Grandparent (1)

- Has the role of grandparent taken over your life?
- Do you have a role model for grandparenting, real or fictitious?
- Have you adopted any grandparenting techniques from your own grandparents?
- Is there an optimum age for becoming a grandparent, or an optimum age gap between grandparent and grandchild?
- Do you have any grandparenting goals?

> **(CN)** The royal road to a man's heart is to talk to him about the things he treasures most. *Dale Carnegie, writer and lecturer.*

- What advice would you give to new grandparents?
- Would grandparenting classes be of interest to you?
- If you have a husband, wife, or partner, do you grandparent as a team?
- Do you feel guilt about any aspects of being a grandparent?
- What should grandparents *not* do in order to avoid embarrassing their grandchildren?

> **(CN)** The first duty of love is to listen. *Paul Tillich, existentialist philosopher and theologian.*

Being a Grandparent (2)

- What was it like the first time you held or met your grandchild?
- Is being a grandparent what you expected?
- What are the different skills you need to be able to deal with your grandchildren as they get older?
- Do you have a difference of opinion with your children over how to parent?
- Are you asked to babysit or look after the children enough? Too much? Not enough?

(CN) The most fruitful and natural exercise for our minds is, in my opinion, conversation. *Michel de Montaigne, French Renaissance writer.*

- As a grandparent, how do you feel about the societal pressures that your grandchildren face?
- Do some grandparents compete for the grandchildren's affection?
- Is it better to have a full life so you are a better-rounded person as a grandparent, or is it better to have as much time as possible to devote to your grandchildren?
- Is there a grandparenting mistake you've made that you wish you could undo?
- What have you discovered about yourself since you became a grandparent? Have you found aspects of yourself you didn't know existed?

(CN) The only reason why we ask other people how their weekend was is so we can tell them about our own weekend. *Chuck Palahniuk, novelist and freelance journalist.*

Being a Grandparent (3)

- If you had to write a job description for the job of "Grandparent," what skills and characteristics would you include?
- What grandparenting role or roles do you play, for example, family historian, disciplinarian, mentor, fun-provider, role model, wise counsel?

- Could you use your skills to help your grandchildren with their hobbies?
- Could you use your skills or knowledge to help your grandchildren with their homework?
- Has your relationship with your child or children changed since you became a grandparent?

(CN) Good communication is as stimulating as black coffee and just as hard to sleep after. *Anne Morrow Lindbergh, aviator.*

- Has your relationship with your husband, wife, or partner changed since you became a grandparent?
- Do you sometimes feel you haven't got enough energy to keep up with the grandchildren?
- Do you sometimes feel out of touch with the kinds of things your grandchildren are interested in?
- Do you remember many of the parenting skills and techniques you used with your own children?
- How much technology do you use in your interactions with your grandchildren?

(CN) There is a world of communication which is not dependent on words. *Mary Martin, actress and singer.*

Grandparent Views (1)

Share your views as a grandparent on the following:

- When babies cry should they always be picked up?
- If a mother isn't sure about bottle feeding her baby, what advice would you give?
- Should girls be treated differently than boys?
- Are there any toys that aren't suitable for young children to play with?
- Should parents start saving for their child's education early on?

(CN) Love without conversation is impossible. *Mortimer Adler, philosopher, educator, and author.*

- Is it OK for babies to sleep in bed with their parents?
- If the parents have different surnames, what surname should the child have?
- Are there any types of food or drink that children shouldn't have?
- How much screen time is it OK for children to have?
- On a scale of 0–10, how strict should parents be?

(CN) Most conversations are simply monologues delivered in the presence of a witness. *Margaret Millar, writer.*

Grandparent Views (2)

- Some people think that maternal grandmothers get a better deal. Do you agree?
- Is it true that grandparenting is easier than parenting, that grandparents have all the fun but without any responsibility?
- If a grandparent has a son whose partner leaves him and takes the children, should the grandparent have access to the grandchildren?
- If a grandparent is very ill, is it OK for the parents to keep the grandchildren away to shield them from the issue, even if the grandparent wants to see them?
- Should both/all sets of grandparents have equal access to the grandchildren for holidays, Christmas, etc.?

(CN) My idea of good company is the company of clever, well-informed people who have a great deal of conversation; that is what I call good company. *Jane Austen, English novelist.*

- Are grandparents generally more easy going with their grand-children than they were with their own children?
- Is it OK for grandparents to have rules for the grandchil-dren in their house that are the opposite of the rules in the parent's house?
- If a grandparent feels a son-in-law or daughter-in-law is treat-ing the children badly and their daughter or son does not agree, should they do anything about it?
- What should a grandparent do if they love their grandchildren deeply but are never left alone with them?
- Is it OK to not like your grandchildren?

(CN) Silence is one of the great arts of conversation. *Marcus Tullius Cicero, Roman philosopher, politician, and orator.*

Your Predictions

- By the next generation, how will grandparents and grandpar-enting be different?
- What will be the next phase in toys for young children?
- Are couples more or less likely to stay together?
- As technology advances, will it have any effect on parenting?
- Will the average age for becoming a parent go up or down?

(CN) A single conversation across the table with a wise person is worth a month's study of books. *Chinese Proverb.*

- Will more grandparents become the primary carers for their grandchildren?
- With many families choosing to relocate, will more grandpar-ents live apart from their grandchildren?
- Will grandparents and senior citizens have more influence in society?
- Will divorce levels increase in older generations?
- Will children become more, or less, respectful of elders?

> **(CN)** Ideal conversation must be an exchange of thought, and not, as many of those who worry most about their shortcomings believe, an eloquent exhibition of wit or oratory. *Emily Post, etiquette author.*

The Things Grandchildren Say

These are typical things that young children say. Do your grandchildren say things like this?

- My granddad says I'm strong and lets me carry heavy things for him.
- My granddad is the cleverest man in the world. I want to be as clever as him.
- My grandma has to take her glasses off and her teeth out at night time.
- Me and my nan have lots of fun together.
- Me and grandma do secret things and don't tell my mom.

> **(CN)** If you're having dinner with a friend and you realize you can't remember what their voice sounds like, you've been talking too much. *Author Unknown.*

- My granddad is so cheeky. He makes me laugh.
- Nanny and Granddad let me have bad food. My mom and dad don't.
- My nana has lots of old things. She has an old teddy bear.
- My granddad lets me comb his hair and put ribbons in it.
- My granddad laughs at all my jokes and plays in the garden with me.

> **(CN)** Conversation would be vastly improved by the constant use of four simple words: I do not know. *André Maurois, French author.*

Then and Now

Compare your childhood to your grandchild's:

- Was it better "back in your day"?
- Do children have it easy these days?

- Are children over-protected now?
- Are children growing up too fast?
- Are children exposed to too much merchandise?

> **(CN)** The more we can get together and talk about various perspectives, feelings, beliefs, the better. *William P. Leahy, college president.*

- Is there more childhood obesity now?
- How does school discipline differ from when you were at school?
- Do children have as much freedom in their environment as you used to have?
- What are children these days missing out on by having so much technology?
- Do children learn the basics at school as well as you did?

> **(CN)** A good conversationalist is not one who remembers what was said, but says what someone wants to remember. *John Mason Brown, drama critic and author.*

What Would You Do?

How would you handle these scenarios?

- Your grandchild accidentally breaks one of your ornaments.
- You find your small grandchild playing "doctors and nurses" with a friend.
- Your young grandchild hits another child in the park.
- Your grandchild says, in front of his parents, that he prefers to be with you rather than them.
- You ask your teenage grandchild to help with some household chores at your house and they swear at you and tell you to leave them alone.

> **(CN)** Conversation has a kind of charm about it, an insinuating and insidious something that elicits secrets just like love or liquor. *Seneca, Roman philosopher, statesman and dramatist.*

- You think your grandchild's parents are far too strict, and are making the child lose confidence.
- One of the grandchild's other grandparents wants to keep the grandchildren to themselves.
- You overhear your son or daughter telling your grandchild to behave well otherwise you will get very angry.
- You think your grandchild may not be developing as they should and the parents don't seem to have noticed.
- You have planned a special evening out and have bought the tickets. At the last minute your daughter calls and says she desperately needs a babysitter and no one else is available.

(CN) Conversation is an exercise of the mind; gossip is merely an exercise of the tongue. *Author Unknown.*

Stereotypes

- What are a stereotypical grandmother and a stereotypical grandfather like?
- Are you a stereotypical grandparent?
- Are you part of a stereotypical family?
- Is blue for a boy and pink for a girl still the norm?
- Do girls still play with dolls and boys play with cars?

(CN) In conversation, humor is worth more than wit and easiness more than knowledge. *George Herbert, poet, orator, and priest.*

- Is there a stereotypical grandparent-parent-grandchild relationship?
- Are there any stereotypical grandparents on TV shows or in films?
- What are the different stereotypical hobbies for boys and girls?
- Is it OK for a man to be a stay-at-home dad?
- Would it be OK for the grandparents to be the main carers, and the parents to play a minor role in child rearing?

> **(CN)** You can design a conversation intentionally, although most people don't. Most conversations have a design that is invisible and unconscious. *Dwight Frindt, businessman and author.*

Protecting Grandchildren

- What are your thoughts about stranger danger?
- Should young children be allowed to take risks such as climbing trees and riding bikes?
- What kinds of films, TV programs, and books are not suitable for young children?
- Should young children have cell phones as a safety measure?
- How do we keep children cyber safe?

> **(CN)** Everything becomes a little different as soon as it is spoken out loud. *Herman Hesse, German poet, novelist, and painter.*

- How can children be protected from playground bullies, text bullies, drugs, and similar negative influences at school?
- Is it a good idea for children to have all the inoculations offered during childhood?
- What is the youngest age at which people should be able to drive?
- If your grandchildren were mixing with other children you felt weren't good influences, what would you do?
- How can we help children avoid obesity?

> **(CN)** All good conversation, manners, and action, come from a spontaneity which forgets usages, and makes the moment great. Nature hates calculators; her methods are saltatory and impulsive. *Ralph Waldo Emerson, essayist, lecturer, and poet.*

Challenging Issues (1)

- What can grandparents do to help single parents?
- How can grandparents help their child and grandchildren through divorce, separation, or loss?

- How can grandparents who are ending a relationship help their grandchild come to terms with this?
- How can grandparents who are starting a new relationship help their grandchild come to terms with this?
- How can grandparents who have had plastic surgery and now look different help their grandchild come to terms with this?

(CN) Mediocre people have an answer for everything and are astonished at nothing. They always want to have the air of knowing better than you what you are going to tell them; when, in their turn, they begin to speak, they repeat to you with the greatest confidence, as if dealing with their own property, the things that they have heard you say yourself at some other place. A capable and superior look is the natural accompaniment of this type of character. *Eugene Delacroix, French Romantic artist.*

- Should grandchildren be shielded from family arguments?
- How can grandparents with significant health issues help their grandchild deal with this?
- Do you feel it's appropriate to talk to your grandchild about when you will no longer be here?
- Is it the grandparent's role to sort out issues between parent and child?
- Can grandparents play a role if their grandchild is bullied at school?

(CN) They are eloquent who can speak of low things acutely, and of great things with dignity, and of moderate things with temper. *Marcus Tullius Cicero, Roman philosopher, politician, and orator.*

Challenging Issues (2)

- Do you think there are things that should be kept from young children, such as attending a funeral, the topic of where babies come from, family rifts, and so on?
- What do you do when your grandchildren behave inappropriately in public?

- Have you had to deal with sibling rivalry?
- Have you had to address the issue of your grandchildren's table manners?
- Do you have a grandchild who is less likeable than the others?

(CN) The art of conversation is the art of hearing as well as of being heard. *William Hazlitt, English writer, social commentator, and philosopher.*

- What would you do if your grandchild told you a significant secret and asked you not to tell their parents?
- What would you do if you found your grandchild stealing something?
- Are you concerned about any of the friends your grandchildren have?
- What challenges do teenage grandchildren present?
- Are your grandchildren too demanding?

(CN) The uses of travel are occasional, and short; but the best fruit it finds, when it finds it, is conversation; and this is a main function of life. *Ralph Waldo Emerson, essayist, lecturer, and poet.*

1–10

On a scale of 1–10, with 1 being the lowest and 10 being the highest, where would you place yourself for:

- Being pretty cool as grandparents go?
- Being a modern grandparent?
- Being a cheeky grandparent?
- Being an educational grandparent?
- Having a full life?

(CN) Most of the successful people I've known are the ones who do more listening than talking. *Bernard M. Baruch, financier, philanthropist, and political consultant.*

- Having a lot of energy?
- Being willing to make a fool of yourself with the grandchildren?
- Understanding children of today?
- Having enough time to spend with grandchildren?
- Being grumpy?

(CN) If you talk to a man in a language he understands, that goes to his head. If you talk to him in his language, that goes to his heart. *Nelson Mandela, South African anti-apartheid revolutionary, politician, and philanthropist.*

Spending Time with Grandchildren

- What's the game or activity you most like doing with your grandchildren?
- What do your grandchildren most like doing with you?
- How often do you see your grandchildren? Is it enough?
- Can you list all the activities you do with your grandchildren?
- Do your grandchildren ever sleep over? What do you prepare in advance?

(CN) Women speak because they wish to speak, whereas a man speaks only when driven to speak by something outside himself—like, for instance, he can't find any clean socks. *Jean Kerr, author and playwright.*

- What's the best surprise you've given your grandchildren?
- Have you bought any items or adapted your house, garden, car, or anything else to accommodate your grandchildren?
- Have you set up any traditions with your grandchildren that will provide them with happy memories?
- Do you act your age when you are with your grandchildren?
- Do you have lots of fun and get up to NO GOOD when you are with them?

(CN) Wisdom is the reward you get for a lifetime of listening when you'd have preferred to talk. *Doug Larson, columnist and editor.*

Marriage

- Does your husband or wife come second to the grandchildren?
- Is it ever too late to get married or remarried?
- Why is there a growing number of "silver splitters"—those over sixty who are divorcing?
- Should parents stay together for the sake of the children?
- Does it make any difference if the children's parents are in a de facto relationship rather than married?

(CN) Speakers who talk about what life has taught them never fail to keep the attention of their listeners. *Dale Carnegie, writer and lecturer.*

- What effect can a grandparent's remarriage have on the rest of the family?
- Does it make a marriage stronger if both partners have their own interests and spend time away from each other?
- Has a book, movie, or TV program ever had an effect on your marriage?
- Do you agree with the part of the vows that say "in sickness and in health, till death do us part"?
- If you marry and become a step-grandparent, what issues might you face?

(CN) When I get ready to talk to people, I spend two thirds of the time thinking what they want to hear and one third thinking about what I want to say. *Abraham Lincoln, 16th President of the United States.*

Aging

- Do you think you look pretty good for your age?
- Do you, or will you, do anything to address the signs of aging?
- When you were younger, did you used to think that people your age were *really* old?
- What do you think of the Bette Davis quote, "Old age ain't no place for sissies"?
- What's your main concern about getting older?

(CN) Be interesting, be enthusiastic... and don't talk too much. *Norman Vincent Peale, author and progenitor of "positive thinking."*

- Do you do anything to keep your brain alert?
- Do you do anything to keep your body working well?
- Have you made any plans for the next phase of your life?
- Do you worry that your grandchildren will miss you once you are gone?
- What legacy would you like to leave behind?

(CN) The great gift of conversation lies less in displaying it ourselves than in drawing it out of others. He who leaves your company pleased with himself and his own cleverness is perfectly well pleased with you. *Jean de La Bruyere, French philosopher.*

Those Special Things

- What names or nicknames have your grandchildren given you?
- Do you have special names for your grandchildren?
- What are some of the most special items your grandchildren have given you or made for you?
- Do you keep items such as gifts or photos of your grandchildren in a special place or in a special way?
- Which is your most precious photo of your grandchildren?

(CN) We spend the first twelve months of our children's lives teaching them to walk and talk and the next twelve telling them to sit down and shut up. *Phyllis Diller, comedienne, actress, and voice artist.*

- Do you make or buy special food or drink for your grandchildren?
- Do you have a different kind of bond with your grandchildren than you had with your children when they were young?
- Do you have any special secret things that only you and your grandchild know about?

- What is something special about your grandchild that makes you proud of them?
- What's the most special treat you have given your grandchild or they have given you?

(CN) The basic rule of human nature is that powerful people speak slowly and subservient people quickly—because if they don't speak fast nobody will listen to them. *Michael Caine, English actor and author.*

Advice Column (1)

The purpose of looking at problems as if you were an advice columnist and being one step removed is to provide the opportunity to work out strategies to deal with challenging issues without having head to head interactions. It could provide you with ways to handle current or future situations.

If any of the issues are similar to your own, you may like to amend the wording.

Imagine you are an advice columnist called Lynsey, who specializes in advising grandparents. People contact you because you give wise and helpful answers. How would you reply to the following?

- Dear Lynsey, I love my daughter very much, but I'm disappointed in her choice of partner. I find him rude, unhelpful, and lazy. Parenting doesn't seem to interest him. He won't change nappies, feed the baby, do the shopping, or any housework. He won't even clean up after their pets; my daughter has to do it all. I see her once a week at the weekend, help her do the shopping, clean around the house, and look after the baby for a couple of hours. She looks very tired and has let her appearance go. I'm concerned for her but don't want to be seen as an interfering mother-in-law. Is there anything I can do to get her husband to help out?
- Dear Lynsey, my son and daughter-in-law and my daughter-in-law's parents all live very close to me. I don't dislike her parents but we have nothing in common, so we only meet up with them at family occasions. Last year, they held an elaborate party for our grandson's birthday which we attended.

This year they want to do the same and my son and his wife have agreed. I think it's our turn, and we would like to host it, even though we wouldn't put on such an extravagant event. What should we do?

- Dear Lynsey, I'm a grandma with three grown-up daughters. The two younger ones have a girl each, and my eldest has a three-year-old boy. Every time I go to visit, my grandson plays with toy guns, and runs around the house shooting at baddies. "Bang bang, you're dead!" he keeps shouting. I don't agree with him having guns at all. I think it will make him turn into a violent teenager, but my daughter won't listen to me when I tell her to take them off him. How can I make her see sense?

- Dear Lynsey, I have six grandchildren ranging in ages from twelve months to nine years. I love them all and want to buy them presents for their birthday and Christmas. However, I'm on a very low income and can't afford very much. Everything the older children want is very expensive, and they don't have any interest in the kinds of things I can afford to buy. I don't want them to think I'm a mean old granddad who doesn't love them. What on earth can I do?

- Dear Lynsey, I hate my granddaughter's other grandparents. They put me and my wife down whenever we see them. They always say things like, "Oh we love our granddaughter very much, that's why we buy her such expensive gifts," or "We'd rather our granddaughter played at our house as ours has a much bigger garden than yours ... and a pool," or "Once she's older I'll get her a good job in my company. I don't suppose you'd be able to do that in *your* job, would you?" I dread family gatherings because I know I'll have to see them, and I hate the thought that my granddaughter is mixing with such revolting people. I need your advice.

(CN) I don't know what he means by that, but I nod and smile at him. You'd be surprised at how far that response can get you in a conversation where you are completely confused. *Jodi Picoult, American author.*

- Dear Lynsey, I can't sleep for crying. In a month's time my daughter and son-in-law will be moving 600 miles away. My son-in-law has been promoted in work and has to go to work at head office. I will miss them and the grandchildren so much. They are such a big part of my life. I'm wondering about moving to live near them but I have a job that I love and all my friends nearby. My heart feels like it's breaking and I'm scared that my heath will suffer. Why do they have to move away and take my grandchildren from me?

- Dear Lynsey, I'm very worried about my daughter. Her older sister has three boys, but my daughter is unable to have children, and she resents family gatherings as she has to face the fact that she is childless. Because of this she doesn't treat the boys in a nice manner and the situation becomes unpleasant. Now her older sister is expecting another baby and things will only get worse. I'm worried for both my daughters and my grandchildren. What can I do to help?

- Dear Lynsey, I have two wonderful teenage grandchildren. The problem is that they don't contact me. I see them when they visit with their mom and dad about once a month, but otherwise I have no contact with them. They won't text me or email me or connect with me on Facebook, even though they spend a lot of time texting their friends when they are at my house. I had a lovely relationship with them when they were younger and now I feel excluded from their life. Am I just being a silly old granny?

- Dear Lynsey, my grandchildren have terrible manners! They don't know how to use a knife and fork properly; they leave the dinner table a mess, never say please and thank you, and expect me to wait on them hand and foot. They are eight and ten years old, and I would expect better behavior from them at these ages. Their parents don't correct them even though they can see what is happening. I don't think it's my job to teach them what to do. Isn't it the parent's job to teach manners? What should I do?

- Dear Lynsey, what does a woman do when her husband starts to behave strangely? Since becoming a grandfather at the age of 65, my husband seems to feel he has lost his youth and is having a mid-life crisis. He has bought trendy clothes, the latest cell phone, and plays computer games a lot. Is this a passing phase or do I need to get help for him?

(CN) The great secret of succeeding in conversation is to admire little, to hear much; always to distrust our own reason, and sometimes that of our friends; never to pretend to wit, but to make that of others appear as much as possibly we can; to hearken to what is said and to answer to the purpose. *Benjamin Franklin, author, politician, scientist, musician, and inventor.*

Advice Column (2)

- Dear Lynsey, my husband and I want to maintain good relations with my son, his wife, and her family, and would like your advice on how to diplomatically deal with the issue I'm facing: My daughter-in-law likes to take my son and grandson to see her parents on a regular basis. I've met her parents several times and they are nice people. However, my son and daughter-in-law visit them about three times more often than they visit us, even though I live the same distance away. My husband and I are feeling excluded and would love to see all three of them on a more regular basis. What can we do?

- Dear Lynsey, my daughter is a single mom to a beautiful five-year-old girl. She is now in a relationship with a new man, but unfortunately this man's parents are very forceful and like to visit my daughter's house most days, and—unbelievably—want a say in how my granddaughter is brought up. They tell her the kinds of clothes the child should wear, what time she should go to bed, and what type of food she should eat. My daughter is quite timid and won't stand up to them even though it is her child's life they are trying to control. Her partner doesn't seem to think there is anything wrong with the situation, as he thinks their advice is sensible. Can you help?

- Dear Lynsey, my son and daughter-in-law have a ten-year-old girl. My daughter-in-law was born in a developing country and moved here a few years ago. Her mother has now come to live with them and sees it as her right to be waited on hand and foot. She shows no love towards my granddaughter, bosses her around, and tries to force her to adopt the culture and religion she was brought up with. My son is livid and argues with his mother-in-law all the time, but to no avail. His wife sees no wrong in what her mother is doing, as that is the way things work in her country. I can see that my granddaughter is unhappy in her own home, but I live two hundred miles away. Is there anything I can do?

- Dear Lynsey, my son was in a relationship for ten years with a woman he didn't like. He stayed because of their child whom he adores. However the relationship became so bad that he had to leave, even though it broke his heart to leave his child. He now lives with me, several hundred miles away from his beloved son. His ex won't let him talk to his son on the phone, has refused to let him go and see him, and says she will throw away any gifts or letters he sends. I believe she would do this. She will, however, accept child support money and becomes very demanding if ever he is late with the payments. She is, and has been, a bad influence on the child. She babies him, feeds him unhealthy food, and over-protects him. Consequently he is very immature and sickly. How do we deal with a bitter, nasty, immature woman?

- Dear Lynsey, my son-in-law and his family have very strong religious beliefs and he would only marry my daughter on the condition that she converted to his religion, which she did. She goes to church and allows the children to go to religious schools simply to keep the peace. Our family members are non-believers. Their oldest girl is now talking about becoming a nun. Her father and his family are very proud but my daughter and I think this has gone too far and we don't want her to throw her life away. How do we tackle this?

(CN) It is through attentive love, the ability to ask, "What are you going through?" and the ability to hear the answer that the reality of the child is both created and respected. *Mary Field Belenky, author.*

- Dear Lynsey, my daughter-in-law's parents like to buy our grandchildren's affections with expensive presents. The grandchildren's house and garden is overflowing with the toys, clothes, books, gadgets, and playground equipment they have bought for them. Twice a year they take them on expensive vacations to Disneyland or some such place. In the beginning we tried to compete by buying lots of gifts, but we no longer want to do this. The grandchildren are becoming spoiled and place no value on the gifts because they have so many. Can we obtain their affection in a different way?

- Dear Lynsey, my daughter married a man from another country. Her husband is becoming increasingly strict in imposing his ways and traditions onto my grandson, which my daughter doesn't agree with. At the back of our minds is the fear that her husband may abduct the child and take him to family in his home country. What preventative measures can we put in place?

- Dear Lynsey, my daughter and her husband adopted a child aged three. His birth mother was a teenager and unable to look after him. My daughter and son-in-law have provided a wonderful life for him and he has been a well-behaved, happy child. However, after twelve years the marriage has ended and my son-in-law has left to live with a woman my grandson doesn't like. At the same time, my grandson discovered that his birth mother has now got her life back on track, has married, and has two children, both of whom live with her. My grandson is feeling rejected: "Why did my dad leave?" "Why did my real mum give me away and keep her other children?" My heart goes out to him. He has given up on school and spends all day at home in his room doing nothing, and all night out with his friends, sometimes not arriving home until the next day. My daughter has been extremely supportive but we are worried that he may go off the rails. What can we do?

- Dear Lynsey, my husband and I sent my (now grown up) daughter to an all-girls boarding school which helped her obtain good qualifications, a good degree, and entry into a top-level career. She would like her son to go to an all-boys board school and I completely agree. I think the standard of education, the life skills, and the contacts he will gain will help him in life immensely. However, my son-in-law fundamentally disagrees with all-boys boarding schools, saying that they foster homosexuality. While my daughter and I can appreciate his concern, we both still feel that an all-boys boarding school is the best option. We only have a short time left before the application needs to be in and are not sure how to proceed.

- Dear Lynsey, my grandchild's other grandparents are more loving, caring, and humorous than we are. We are much more down to earth, practical, and pragmatic. We love our grandchildren and show our love by buying educational gifts and making things for them. We don't like a lot of hugging and kissing but are happy to sit and converse with our grandchildren or make things with them. However, this means that the grandchildren want to spend more time with their other grandparents who hug and kiss them and laugh a lot. We feel a little rejected. We know we can't compete but still want to spend time with the grandchildren, so what can we do?

(CN) If family communication is good, parents can pick up the signs of stress in children and talk about it before it results in some crisis. If family communication is bad, not only will parents be insensitive to potential crises, but the poor communication will contribute to problems in the family. *Donald C. Medeiros, author.*

Advice Column (3)

Dealing with more challenging issues:
- Dear Lynsey, I'm ashamed to say this, but my son hits his children. They are just being boisterous young children, but he thinks they need to be disciplined. It breaks my heart to see it happening. His wife doesn't hit them but nor does she stop my son from doing it. How can I help them?
- Dear Lynsey, my son-in-law is having an affair; my daughter is devastated and is not coping very well. She is holding onto the hope that they can reconcile. Yesterday I was at their house

when their 10 year old said to me, "Why is mommy crying?" I didn't know what to say. How can I deal with this sensitively?

- Dear Lynsey, we have a teenage grandson who has dropped out of high school and refuses to get a job. The problem is that his other grandfather gives him money, saying, "I'm just helping the poor kid." His mom and dad are struggling to make ends meet and so are happy that the grandfather gives money. We think that bailing him out is doing more harm than good and our grandson will never learn to stand on his own two feet. Should we say something?

- Dear Lynsey, yesterday I was at the shopping mall with my two young grandchildren. I have mobility issues and was struggling to get round. A young male started imitating the way I walk while he and his mates laughed. Then he said, "People like you shouldn't be allowed out." I was mortified that the grandchildren had to witness it; they should never be allowed to see such a lack of respect. If this kind of thing happens again, what's the best way to deal with it?

- Dear Lynsey, my daughter remarried recently after a difficult first marriage and a whirlwind romance. She is infatuated with her new husband and can see no wrong in him, but I have doubts. I look after the children when they finish school and they tell me they don't like him, and ask me not to leave them alone with him because he shouts at them. What should I do?

(CN) You're talking about a younger generation, Generation Y, whose interpersonal communication skills are different from Generation X. The younger generation is more comfortable saying something through a digital mechanism than even face to face. *Erik Qualman, author of Socialnomics.*

- Dear Lynsey, I am at my wits' end. My son and his partner refuse to let me see my grandchildren because they don't think I'm a "suitable influence" on the children. I can't understand what they mean because I love the children very much. What can I do?

- Dear Lynsey, my husband and I have been married for too long. We shouldn't be together as we have no love left for each other, but financially we need to live in the same house. We argue all the time and I hate that the grandchildren have to experience our arguments, but my husband irritates me so much that I can't stop. I'm worried about the effect it has on the grandchildren and I'm worried that their parents may not want them to visit us. Please give your advice.
- Dear Lynsey, how can we prepare our grandchildren for coping with my wife's condition? She has dementia and is becoming progressively worse.
- Dear Lynsey, the most awful thing has happened. My son is in the army and has been killed while on duty overseas. He leaves a beautiful wife and two young children who are just old enough to realize that he will not be coming back. The sense of grief and loss in their household is overwhelming and we want to make sure we offer the right kind of support.
- Dear Lynsey, how is it possible to cope with the death of a grandchild? We suffer so much every day, and yet we need to be strong for the sake of my son and daughter-in-law.

(CN) The level of communication you can achieve with an infant is really profound.
Mayim Bialik, actress

Lessons

If you wanted to teach your grandchildren these lessons, how would you do it?
- You want to teach them how to spend pocket money wisely, and not rush out and spend it on the first thing they think of.
- You want to teach them to have respect for people who are different to them.
- You want to teach them that it's OK to try new things and not get them right first time.
- You want to teach them that not everything brings rewards in the short term and that good things take time.
- You want to teach them how to be empathetic.

(CN) Constantly talking isn't necessarily communicating. *Charlie Kaufman, screenwriter and lyricist.*

- You want to teach them how to be grateful.
- You want to teach them that it's OK to show their emotions.
- You want to teach them that they will be good at some things in life and not others, and not to feel inferior about things they are not naturally good at.
- You want to teach them that if they are bored, there are many things they can find to do.
- You want to teach them to respect their elders.

(CN) Ultimately, it is the receiving of the child and hearing what he or she has to say that develops the child's mind and personhood. Parents who enter into a dialogue with their children, who draw out and respect their opinions, are more likely to have children whose intellectual and ethical development proceeds rapidly and surely. *Mary Field Belenky, author.*

Travel

- Have you been on vacation with your grandchildren?
- What would be the best educational trip you could take your grandchildren on?
- What has been your best vacation ever?
- Have you got any travel plans for the coming year?
- If you could plan a perfect vacation, where would you go, who would you go with, how long would you go for, and what would you do?

(CN) Think like a wise man but communicate in the language of the people. *William Butler Yeats, Irish poet and senator.*

- Which modes of travel do you like, planes, trains, cars, ships, cycles, motorcycles, other?
- What is your favorite type of accommodation?

- Do you prefer relaxing vacations or more adventurous ones?
- How do you choose which type of trip to have?
- Do you travel much with your job or business?

(CN) Feelings of worth can flourish only in an atmosphere where individual differences are appreciated, mistakes are tolerated, communication is open, and rules are flexible—the kind of atmosphere that is found in a nurturing family. *Virginia Satir, author and psychotherapist.*

Money

NOTE: Please be considerate when using this topic; it may be a sensitive area for some people. Check it's OK to talk about these issues.

- What are some of the most beneficial ways to use money?
- What are non-beneficial ways to use money?
- Is money an emotional issue for you?
- What do you think of the concept of "SKI"ing, an acronym for "Spending the Kids' Inheritance," where parents use all their retirement savings rather than passing them on?

(CN) Words calculated to catch everyone may catch no one. *Adlai E. Stevenson politician.*

- How will you—or do you—manage financially when you are no longer working?
- Are your finances in order for the next part of your life?
- What are your thoughts on paying off a mortgage?
- Have you made any major purchases you regret?
- Do you make use of senior discounts?
- If you do a sizeable amount of child care, would you expect your children to pay?

(CN) Communication is about being effective, not always about being proper. *Bo Bennett, entrepreneur.*

Work and Business

- What are the challenges in finding a job when you are older?
- Do you have any tips for writing a CV when you are older?
- Which organizations employ and value older workers?
- What's a good type of work for older people?
- What factors might a business owner have to take into account if they were hoping to pass the business over to their child or grandchild?

(CN) Great conversation ... requires an absolute running of two souls into one. *Ralph Waldo Emerson, essayist, lecturer, and poet.*

- What are suitable types of jobs or businesses you can do from home?
- What are easy ways to make extra income alongside a job?
- Is it a good idea to set up a business when you are near retirement age?
- What factors need to be taken into account and what plans need to be made as people head towards retirement?
- For people who are bored in retirement, what kinds of work or voluntary work might be suitable?

(CN) Even though friends say they are interested in your life, they never really want to talk about you as much as you want them to. *Charise Mericle Harper, author.*

Fun!

- What's your idea of a great day out?
- What's your idea of a great night out?
- Do you like parties?
- Tell us about the best party you've been to.
- What kinds of fun things happen at your family gatherings?

(CN) When you speak, ask questions. Don't lecture. *Denis Waitley, author.*

- If money were no object, what other hobbies or activities would you do?
- Who or what makes you laugh?
- If you were going to plan a surprise birthday treat for one of your friends, what would you organize?
- You have been invited to a fancy dress party and have to go dressed as a TV or cartoon character. Would you go, and if so, who would you go as?
- One of your friends is getting remarried at the age of 65 and wants you to organize a fun hen night/stag do. What would you organize?

(CN) Keep the other person's well-being in mind when you feel an attack of soul-purging truth coming on. *Betty White, actress, singer, author, and television personality.*

Males and Females

- Studies show that some differences between boys and girls are evident from an early age. For example girls are more in tune with people's emotions and start talking earlier; while boys have better spatial skills, like to run, play ball and jump more than girls and are more physically aggressive. Have you noticed any differences in boys' and girls' development?
- Are mixed gender schools better than single sex schools?
- Do girls tend to get on better with their mother and boys get on better with their father?
- What do you think of momma's boys and daddy's girls?
- Is there an age at which children are happy to play with children of either gender?

(CN) The most basic and powerful way to connect to another person is to listen. Just listen. Perhaps the most important thing we ever give each other is our attention.... A loving silence often has far more power to heal and to connect than the most well-intentioned words. *Rachel Naomi Remen, author and teacher.*

- What differences might there be in a family with two boys, a family with two girls, and a family with a boy and a girl?
- What's the difference between toys and books for boys, and toys and books for girls?
- Is it ever too early for a child to have a girlfriend or boyfriend?
- Do boys and girls learn differently?
- Does society have any rites of passage to help girls transition to womanhood and boys transition to manhood?

(CN) Communication leads to community, that is, to understanding, intimacy and mutual valuing. *Rollo May, existential psychologist.*

Reading

- Have you read any books on grandparenting?
- Do you use any grandparent websites?
- Do you read to your grandchildren?
- Do children read enough these days?
- What was your favorite childhood book?

(CN) The real art of conversation is not only to say the right thing at the right place but to leave unsaid the wrong thing at the tempting moment. *Dorothy Nevill, English writer, hostess, and horticulturist.*

- How often do you read a newspaper and which one do you mainly read?
- Do you read any magazines?
- What types of books do you read?
- Do you ever buy books or get them from the library and then not read them?
- What do you think of e-readers?

(CN) One way to prevent conversation from being boring is to say the wrong thing. *Frank Sheed, lawyer, writer, publisher, and speaker.*

Your Favorites & Your Starters

Here you can make a note of any of your favorite starters, and compile a list of your own questions and conversation starters.

FAVORITE STARTERS

MY OWN QUESTIONS AND CONVERSATION STARTERS

KEEPSAKE MEMORIES

In this section you can make a note of the interesting points and stories that come out of your conversations, and keep them as a memory.

Date	Conversation with ...	Memories

Date	Conversation with ...	Memories

Date	Conversation with ...	Memories

Date	Conversation with ...	Memories